INTO THE UNKNOWN

MORE THAN EYE CAN SEE

P.M. Stuebe

pmstuebe.com

Into the Unknown

More Than Eye Can See

P. M. STUEBE

First Edition

First Printing, 2013

ISBN-13: 978-1482347883

ISBN-10: 1482347881

For permission requests, please contact the author via email provided below:
pmstuebe@gmail.com

- Table of Contents -

For anyone who is now facing, or has ever faced, an unknown.
Within these pages, may you find encouragement and illumination.

- PREFACE -

In writing this book, it is my deepest hope that you, the reader, would find greater purpose for your own life. In the mundane, that you would see opportunity; in seemingly insignificant moments, that the light of destiny would shine forth. Through pain, sorrow and darkness, that you would be illumined to a truth that would set you free. Free to live your life according to a purpose greater than you can imagine.

There is so much more to life than meets the eye—beyond what can be seen. It is the very truth therein that beckons us to search for purpose. And, when we find it, there is much reason for rejoicing! Not only does finding one's purpose in life result in a greater joy than can be described fully, the experience also fans into flame the desire for making the most out of seemingly menial days.

Though issues of faith—the origins of the universe, relationship with the Creator, believing for the unseen and so on—

are complex to say the least; it is with simplicity that they must be approached. What I mean is this: Jesus said, "I am telling you, once and for all, that unless you return to square one and start over *like children*, you're not even going to get a look at the kingdom, let alone get in." (Mt 18:3; MSG)

Basically, if we desire to discover the great mysteries of the universe and of our very own existence, we must approach this process in a simplistic, childlike manner. It is vital to note that not only is the childlike approach simple, it is also humble and dependent. In order to be illumined to the greatest truths, we must be humble enough to accept that which we do not fully understand, and that which may contradict our own opinions and preferences, likes and dislikes.

This, I believe, is why in the writing of this book, I felt prompted to use many stories from my childhood—when I was pondering great questions to which I had no means of comprehending. It is in many of these simplistic childhood contemplations that some of my most revelatory thoughts have been birthed. What started in seed-form has now come to fruition. May the fruit of my own life serve as nourishment to yours.

As a disclaimer, I do not intend to give the impression in any way that I have answers to all or even most of the questions about life and faith. My purpose in writing this is not to present myself as some sort of spiritual guru; it is simply to share my heart and any wisdom I've received, acquired through a combination of study and personal life experiences. In the footsteps of a foremost influential writer to me, Philip Yancey, I write simply to answer some of my own questions about life and faith.

I do not want people to view this book as some sort of didactic doctrinal reference, but rather more like a story, poem or song, in the sense that I do not intend to approach you as a professor or preacher, but rather an artist and friend. With this being my spoken premise, I now invite you to join me on a journey, to travel the landscapes of thought, emotion and revelation. To set out on a quest for greater understanding, and to attain a new appreciation for those things, which are now and may always be, mystery.

> "There is very little we know for sure. Even the truths we hold of God's creation, our fall and redemption, are claimed by faith, not proof. Our best hope is for momentary glimpses of understanding. The more we learn, the greater our unknowing. Laws of nature, like gravity or the turning earth, or electromagnetic fields are facts; but even these we cannot fully comprehend."
>
> -Carol J. Rottman, Ph.D, *Writers in the Spirit*[1]

- Chapter One -

Childhood Ponderings

"When I was a child, I talked like a child,

I thought like a child, I reasoned like a child."

-1 Corinthians 13:11 (NIV)

- Chapter One -

Childhood Ponderings

I can't remember the weather that day, or how the subject matter came to such. As a matter of fact, I cannot even tell you what my exact age was. Although, I can guess I was probably around the age of ten years. All that I can recall with certainty is that I was quite adamant regarding my sudden conclusion. Somewhere in that two-story house, which sat at the very middle of a cul-de-sac on 52nd and Golden, I approached my mother with my thesis-of-sorts.

"Mom, T.V. isn't real!" I declared so boldly yet with an air of total confusion. Kids have a way of doing that.

She then proceeded to request a more complete explanation for my statement, most likely quite curious as to why I had interrupted her train of thought with such a wild proclamation.

"Well," I continued, "It just doesn't make any sense! Pictures cannot come from wires!"

She patiently waited as I continued my dissertation.

"And, phones and radios aren't real either. Sound also can't come out of wires!"

Though I seemed so clear and solid on my conclusion that day, my statements of revelation were merely spoken out of utter frustration with not being able to understand my subject matter. I'm certain my mother thought it at least somewhat amusing that I was so boldly deciding, and declaring to the world, that T.V. wasn't real. But the truth of the matter was, I had no idea what I was talking about! Of course T.V. is real. I mean, you can touch it, turn it on, you can even break it—as I liked to do with many things at that age.

What I was grappling with, which I didn't know at the time, was that sometimes things in life are just impossible to fully understand. Certain things we learn over time, and others, well, we never really totally understand. I'll admit, I still don't really know how pictures and sound travel through wires and circuit boards.

They just do. Even today, as an adult, when I think too deeply about how this is even possible, my brain begins to hurt. So, I try not to think about it too much; rather, I simply enjoy the benefits of this mysterious travel of picture and sound through my computer, television, and car stereo. Just because I have no clue how it accomplishes its mission of travelling from point A to point B, doesn't mean I can't simply enjoy it.

This, in essence, is the purpose for the pages presented before you now. In writing this book it is my goal to help both you and I come to grips with the fact that there are many things we cannot understand at the moment, and though many of these things will accumulate clarity throughout our years lived on earth, likewise many of them will remain entirely mysterious—and that is okay. We don't have to fully comprehend how the thing works in order to enjoy the benefits of it. C.S. Lewis said:

> "You may ask what good it will be to us if we do not understand it. But that is easily answered. A man can eat his dinner without understanding exactly how food nourishes him. A man can accept what Christ has done without understanding how it works: indeed, he certainly

would not know how it works until he accepted it." [2]

Thus is also true about life. There is much to learn, and what a wonderful journey of knowledge it is to discover and receive greater understanding of the clockwork therein. Yet, there is also great excitement and adventure within all the unknowns of life. Whether we one day find out what purpose they held, or not.

The Revelations Continue

I can remember another day similar to that of my T.V. discovery. My mother and I were sitting in our maroon colored Plymouth minivan just outside our local Arby's restaurant devouring some delicious thin sliced beef burgers with extra Arby's sauce. I had just finished declaring, ever so boldly yet again, that if I couldn't be with this particular girl I liked at school, I would never be with anyone else! I was quite serious too, almost as serious as when I had protested television's validity. As she so often did, with her patience and abundant motherly wisdom, she gently encouraged me to be a little more open to the idea that this girl wasn't my only option for a future wife—all the while chuckling here and there between words at the hilarity of my statement. My middle school mind was too *advanced* for that however, and I held my ground. She *was* the "one"! So, with my firm conclusion to that matter, and thoroughly disregarding my mother's wise counsel, we moved on to the next topic.

Something had been brewing in me for a while that I couldn't quite wrap my mind around. And this area of interest was much more out of my league than television sets and girls—even though females are a mystery that males may never fully understand, and that too, is okay. No, this topic of discussion and personal contemplation was much more "out there" than anything I had ever brought up in a conversation with anyone, even my mother.

"Mom," I said somewhat hesitantly, probably wiping some Arby's sauce off my lip as the words tumbled out.

"Who am I? I don't know if *I'm* real!" I could see the curiosity grow stronger as she stared at me intently.

"I mean, sometimes it feels like I'm not me; it's like I'm someone else, looking out of my body like I'm in a submarine or something and I'm just seeing the world through a periscope."

The past few weeks I had been feeling this way, becoming more and more aware of this strange phenomenon. Sometimes I would just sit there and stare off into space, thinking deeply about how my body maybe wasn't real, and the real me was on the inside. Little did I know at the time, but I wasn't the only one who experienced this. In all actuality, I think most people have, at least at times, felt something similar to my strange revelation. Though I can't recall exactly what my mother said in response to this dilemma, I'm sure she had some great words of insight and encouragement as she reminded me of what the Bible said on this subject. Even so, it's something I never began to understand until a few years ago. And, much like the complications of sounds and pictures travelling through little metal wires and green pieces of flat plastic, it is an area of which much understanding is still lacking.

Something More

In thinking through these memories of my childhood, I am reminded that things aren't always what they seem. There is a substance *behind* everything we see, from the intricacies of the inner workings of computers, to the even more baffling—and seemingly magical—complexities of a garden-variety plant. There is a certain meaning and origin to everything we experience in life. We often simply become comfortable with life as usual and fail to see beyond the obvious. But I think if we were to be honest with ourselves, we have all asked questions about the greater meaning to it all. Matthew Dickerson very eloquently put it in this way:

> "...There are invisible principles at work, and they concern us immensely. They should not be taken as mere ideas to be toyed with. If they are true, these ideas are perhaps the most significant that we can imagine, and should be dwelt upon: the idea that there is a personal God who can be understood as both supremely just and unendingly loving; the idea that there is more to our existence than meets the eye; the possibility of angels, and powers that cannot be controlled by us, and that are subservient to greater powers still; the idea of a war between good and evil in a world parallel to ours—these ideas.... translate the invisible into the practical." [3]

"Why am I here? Of what purpose do I go about day in and day out? Is there more to life than just living? Or, yet, am I even *living* at all?" From what I have learned through my own life, and what others—wiser and greatly more knowledgeable than myself—have taught me, there is definitely a reason for everything. Like a great story being told behind each sunset and sunrise. You may, like me, have been struck with the sensation of looking out of your own body as if you were someone else entirely. And, then again, maybe you haven't. Nonetheless, I think it is valid to assume that this thought brings a certain curiosity to your mind: a longing to find out more about yourself, more about the world around you, and the origins of both. For it is within the very origins of life that we find purpose.

- Chapter Two -

The Unseen You

"Every ant knows the formula of its ant-hill, every bee knows the formula of its beehive. They know it in their own way… Only humankind does not know its own formula."

–Fyodor Dostoyevsky[4]

- Chapter Two -

The Unseen You

Grey hair, weak knees, back pains, endless trips to the doctor's office, wrinkles, loss of memory, senility—we all, I can safely assume, are plenty aware of what growing old entails. These physical bodies of ours aren't made to last. The older we become, the more they break down. Unfortunately, many people wait far too long to reflect on this fact. You don't need to be seventy-plus years advanced in order to ponder the deeper meaning of life. Yet, this is how it often plays out. And, even sadder to behold, is the person well advanced in years who has obviously not even begun to walk in a greater understanding of the meaning of life.

There is more to you than meets the eye. Obviously, as we just discussed, the human body will not last. No matter how many vitamins, medications, medical treatments, self-help books and naturopathic studies one partakes of in an attempt to maximize the extent of their chronological life, the truth is, it simply will not last. One day, your physical body will break down and die.

Inner-Body Experiences

Let's revisit my story of childhood, when I had those big questions and strange thoughts. Pondering whether electronic objects were real—whether even, I myself was real. The latter question, about my own tangibility, is the one I would like to discuss at present.

I remember how confused I was. Every time the thought came back, I would simply sit and daze into nothingness, contemplating over and over this strange sensation. I've heard of people having out of body experiences before, but this was reversed, like an "inner-body" experience! I couldn't get over the strangeness of it. Feeling as if this life I was living was meaningless, as if the world around me was simply an illusion and I was trapped within the mirage.

Being just a young boy, I hadn't nearly enough knowledge and problem-solving ability to figure this one out. And so, I left it alone for years and years. Whenever it would present itself again, I would either enjoy the moment of mystery, or try not to think about it at all. As the years went by, I remember becoming even less fond of trying to solve this mystery. It was most likely because, through some particularly rebellious years of my life, I had come to greatly dislike anything having to do with God, the Bible, and most of all Jesus Christ.

There was a period of time when I wanted nothing whatsoever to do with the faith of my parents, and I did anything not to think about the way I was living my life, in light of what the Bible said about how I *should* be living. It made me feel guilty for the choices I was making. I didn't like that feeling. And, this occasional occurrence ("inner-body" experience) caused thoughts to roam my mind of "something more." It brought up questions of who I was, and that led to other questions of, "Why am I here? How did I get here?"...And so on. So, you can see, as much of an anti-Christian as I was, during that period of my life, I didn't much care for my "inner-body" experiences anymore.

Piecing it Together

It wasn't until about seven years ago that I began to really reflect on this phenomenon, and find out what purpose it served in my life. I emerged from the worldly lifestyle I had been living for several years, got involved in a good local Christian church and began reading the Bible. Then after a short period of time, when these strange "inner-body" experiences weren't happening very often anymore, I started pondering the occurrences once again. This time 'round however, I had a lot of help! I was now in a good community of Christian believers, actually conversing with my parents, and was praying and reading Scripture nearly every day. I now had the necessary environment and tools at my disposal to interpret these mysterious moments.

It then began to make perfect sense: why I felt like I was someone else looking out of my own body; why it seemed like the *real* me was on the inside, and my body was just a vessel—a casing, shell, robot suit or something else. You see, what I found out was that the Bible had been holding the answers all along. Now don't be afraid, I assure you my intention is not to thump you on the head with a big black Bible. Yet, the truth is, the Bible *is the truth.* It is what helped me to learn answers to the toughest questions I've ever faced, and it is certainly true that I am not the only one. So, with that out of the way, shall we continue? Let's go back to the very beginning—the beginning of time—and correspondingly, the beginning of the Bible.

> Then the LORD God formed a man from the dust of the ground and *breathed into his nostrils the breath of life*, and the man became a living being.
>
> -Genesis 2:7 (NIV; *italics mine*)

It is quite remarkable that man was the only piece of God's creation into which He breathed. The animals did not have this direct breath from God, and neither did the vegetation. Only man received the individually unique breath of God into him, bringing him to life. The most common use of the word *breath* in the Bible when used in the spiritual sense is the Greek word *pneúma*—or Hebrew *rûaḥ*, if in the Old Testament—which means, spirit. [5]

Mankind, then, is unique. We are the only ones who have a spirit, the sole beings that bear the ability inside of us to connect relationally with our Creator. All other creation is simply bound to oblivious instinctual behavior, whilst we can speak with, walk with and get to know on a personal basis, the One who has designed our frame. This sheds much light on the subject of who we are and why we are here on earth. God breathed into us a spirit so that we could have the ability to be relational with Him. Thus, we must look more to the "inner-man" (or woman) in order to better understand who we really are, and what this life is all about. As another Scripture says:

> But it is the *spirit* in a man, the *breath of the Almighty*, that gives him understanding.
>
> –Job 32:8 (NIV)

That Which Lasts

"We complain about death and time…there is never enough time. Time makes being into non-being. Time is a river that takes away everything it brings: nations, civilizations, art, science, culture, plants, animals, our own bodies, the very stars—nothing stands outside this cosmic stream rushing headlong into the sea of death.

Or does it? Something in us seems to stand outside it, for something in us protests this 'nature' and asks: Is this all there is? We find this natural situation 'vanity': empty, frustrating, wretched, unhappy. Our nature contradicts nature."

-Peter Kreeft[6]

We all know how fleeting this physical existence—one lifespan—is, even if I make a name for myself that people will remember for years to come. How does it benefit me at all, if people remember my name and legacy for decades after my passing, if I myself do not "pass" into fulfillment? I think it is safe to assume you have at least an idea of what I'm referring to. Heaven is real, and so is Hell. We will discuss these great unknowns in further detail in the coming chapters. Right now, however, we are focusing on you, and me.

What are you making of your life at this very moment? This is a crucial question that should continually cross your mind. Is your focus continually drawn to the temporal? That which you can feel, taste, touch and see? Whether you are a Christian or not, I think it is safe to assume that we all grapple with this. It is much easier to invest our attentions in that which is obvious. These aspects of life are so real to us because they are thrust into our line of sight twenty-four-seven. Our need for food, water, clothing, cleaning, work, play, and so on.

Don't get me wrong; all of the things I've just listed, and many that I haven't, are not bad in and of themselves, and are even essential to a healthy life. However, if this is as far as our ponderings go, we are to be pitied indeed. We need to take the trek into the deeper regions of understanding, peeling back the veil of our so-called reality, to see beyond that which is so obvious to us. And, this exercise does not always require stepping away from those daily tasks and endeavors. As a matter of fact, it is even more rewarding at times to reflect on the eternal aspects of life while in the midst of menial activities. For it is important that we do not completely separate the two—temporal and eternal—in our minds. The revelation that "that-which-lasts" is our inner-self should be motivation to think more purposefully in all aspects of life. Faith is not a safety net waiting to catch us when we die; it is the power by which we can walk in hope and purpose every day. In denying ourselves the privilege of walking in "that-which-lasts," we rob from our own destiny and squander a great wealth.

Many people spend their entire lives investing in that-which-does-not-last: whether it is building themselves into the most professional and powerful businessman or businesswoman, or developing a new line of cosmetics, or spending all their time mulling over volumes of literature. Although these endeavors we put our hands and heart to in life can be very noble, rewarding, and even greatly impact the positive development of others' lives, it all comes to an abrupt stop when life is over. And only then will we see how lasting our toil really was. The only way there will be lasting meaning to anything we do in this life is if we are illumined to what is eternal, and live every day within that light. If our spirit is truly the only part of us that will live on after our temporal physical life is over, we must invest our efforts there. We must deposit all our wealth into the savings account of the Eternal. You would never invest your money in a bank with a shady reputation, would you? Then, why would you invest your life in a fading philosophy, knowing in the end you will have nothing to show for your labor?

I'm sure you have heard the jingle, "You can't take it with you." Well, it's true. I've heard of people asking to be buried with their prized possessions, such as a grown man wanting to be buried with his motorcycle! This is ignorance. It's just going to stay in the ground and rot, like the rest of all earthly things. You really *can't* take it with you. As Job said,

> Naked I came from my mother's womb, and naked I will depart.
>
> –Job 1:21 (NIV)

We spend far too much time focusing on the things that do not last. On possessions, pleasures, momentary satisfaction. All the while missing out on the more lasting and fulfilling elements available to us.

Seek First

God, as our Maker, also desires to be our sole Provider. Scripture says,

> "And why do you worry about clothes? See how the flowers of the field grow. They do not labor or spin. Yet I tell you that not even Solomon in all his splendor was dressed like one of these. If that is how God clothes the grass of the field, which is here today and tomorrow is thrown into the fire, will he not much more clothe

> you—you of little faith? So do not worry, saying, 'What shall we eat?' or 'What shall we drink?' or 'What shall we wear? For the pagans run after all these things, and your heavenly Father knows that you need them. But seek first his kingdom and his righteousness, and all these things will be given to you as well."
>
> –Matthew 6:28-34 (NIV)

Does this not make it clear, that He wants to provide for all of our needs? And, doesn't that only make sense? He is ultimately our Father after all. We are His children. A good earthly father provides and cares for the needs of his children. How much more God, our Heavenly Father, desires to bless us, His children. He wants to free us of the great concern and worry we have for making all the ends meet, and all for the purpose of drawing us closer to Him. This is incredible: to know that God, who breathed His breath of life into us, who gave us a spirit and the ability—above all other creation—to be in personal relationship with Him, wants us to trust Him to provide for all of our needs. And with this truth, what a great weight is lifted from our chests. What great purpose it speaks into our days on earth.

Let us continually turn our focus from the temporal to the Eternal, from what is obvious, to what is unseen. Let us beseech the One who knows all the answers, the One with whom we have the ability to personally connect through the unique spirit He gave us. May we pause to consider how our lives are more than what we can see with mortal eyes, and allow the Eternal to invade our most mundane of days.

This is what Jesus did. He always focused on the more eternal aspects of life and, in turn, caused others to do the same. There are a couple of stories in particular that come to mind. In both stories, we see that there is more to life than food and drink. Jesus wanted us to see that what is more important is to focus on our relationship with the Creator—the only one who can provide for our needs, both physically and spiritually. This is an excerpt from the story of the Woman at the Well:

> When a Samaritan woman came to draw water, Jesus said to her, "Will you give me a drink?" (His disciples had gone into the town to buy food.) The Samaritan woman said to him, "You are a Jew and I am a Samaritan woman. How can you ask me for a drink?" (For Jews do not associate with Samaritans.) Jesus answered her,

> "If you knew the gift of God and who it is that asks you for a drink, you would have asked him and he would have given you living water." "Sir," the woman said, "you have nothing to draw with and the well is deep. Where can you get this living water? Are you greater than our father Jacob, who gave us the well and drank from it himself, as did also his sons and his livestock?" Jesus answered, "Everyone who drinks this water will be thirsty again, but whoever drinks the water I give them will never thirst. Indeed, the water I give them will become in them a spring of water welling up to eternal life."
>
> -John 4:7-14 (NIV)

And just a few verses after this we see Jesus talking in the same way about the difference between natural and spiritual, temporal and eternal.

> They came out of the town and made their way toward him. Meanwhile his disciples urged him, "Rabbi, eat something." But he said to them, "I have food to eat that you know nothing about."

> Then his disciples said to each other, "Could someone have brought him food?" "My food," said Jesus, "is to do the will of him who sent me and to finish his work."
>
> -John 4:30-34 (NIV)

In both of these stories—which actually are simply different parts of the same story—the message is clear, that material food and water (essentials of physical life) are not nearly as important as spiritual food and water, and should be held in right perspective. Is it not unsurprising that the woman at the well was simply concerned with the physical, temporal water? And even the disciples, being concerned with Jesus' need for proper nutrition, wasn't uncanny. These are, after all, necessities of life. Jesus was in no way suggesting that we should neglect our need for food and fluids; He was simply calling us to look beyond. To be more focused on that which lasts. We were made for more than filling our bellies.

- Chapter Three -

Conversations with the Creator

The mingled, mingling threads of life are woven by warp and woof: calms crossed by storms, a storm for every calm. There is no steady unretracing progress in this life; we do not advance through fixed gradations, and at the last one pause: — through infancy's unconscious spell, boyhood's thoughtless faith, adolescence' doubt (the common doom), then scepticism, then disbelief, resting at last in manhood's pondering repose of If. But once gone through, we trace the round again; and are infants, boys, and men, and Ifs eternally. Where lies the final harbor, whence we unmoor no more? In what rapt ether sails the world, of which the weariest will never weary?

-Herman Melville, Moby Dick[7]

- Chapter Three -

Conversations with the Creator

It was a crisp, cold morning, from what I can recall. As I began my descent of the sky-high stairs, departing dormitory number four of Portland Bible College, there was somewhat of a hop in my step. For some reason, I felt that this day held something special just for me.

Of course, just about any time that I had scheduled meetings with one of my mentors, there was a certain expectancy that would overtake me. On this particular morning I was meeting with Rich Miller, the Dean of Students at PBC. He had spoken very purposefully into my life before, resulting in my personal growth, and somehow I knew, that today's conversation time would follow suit.

With the mountainous tower of stairs now behind me, I continued on my brief trek down to the administration building. I strolled past the line of distinctive student vehicles, snugly parked against the curb of the long sidewalk. And just past this, overlooking the lawn sat the other three student dorms—one of them being the other guys' dorm, and the other two for the girls. These other dorms, as different as they were from mine—which was high atop the hill, and much more simple in design—have always grabbed my attention. Their structure bearing elements similar to that of medieval times sends my mind on a journey of epic thought. I can almost envision archers perched in the parapets adorning each building, ready and poised with their bowstrings drawn, to eliminate oncoming attackers.

Alas, this was my imagination running wild, and I hadn't any time for daydreams at the moment. I was in quite the hurry to arrive for my meeting early, as was my tradition. Almost there, I scurried down the steep-sloped sidewalk to the door of the admin building. As I grabbed the handle and turned with a swift rotation of my wrist, the door flung open with a swish, then slammed shut with a somewhat muffled thud behind me as I entered. Once inside, I walked to the sitting area arrayed with aesthetically pleasing décor and quite comfortable furniture. In a way it resembled a cozy living room. The towering receptionist counter just next to this however, brought me back to the reality it was in fact an office building.

As usual, I was early and Mr. Miller was not yet in office. So, I proceeded to retrieve an old yearbook from the bookshelf beside the couch, and began flipping through the pages. Gazing at the pictures of the students who had come and gone before me, I couldn't help but be inspired. It was almost as if they were all coaching me on, encouraging me in my own academic journey. My time of reminiscent reflection was short-lived however, when just then as I looked through the glass panes of the door I had entered moments ago, I could see Mr. Miller approaching.

"He's late." I thought to myself while rising from my chair to greet him. I have always been, after all, overly punctual.

We walked down the hallway and entered his office, immediately taking our seats. I sat on the couch, and he at his desk just adjacent to it—leaning to the edge of it every now and again as we spoke, to show his attentive involvement in our conversation. We talked about an array of basic subjects: school, work, vision, girls. Then, he asked me a question that really struck a chord.

He asked, "How is your relationship with God? How is your devotional life?"

To which I replied, honestly, "It could be better."

He then continued by asking me what I thought was most important in regard to my relationship with God. In response, I tried to be as honest as possible while scavenging my mind for the most theological answer. I was, after all, a Bible college student and aspiring to be a pastor. Out came a spiel of sporadic answers flowing from my mind, which at the moment felt like scrambled eggs. I was being put on the spot unexpectedly and early in the morning at that. He waited patiently for me to finish, and then, seeing how I wasn't following on the same page as he, began his exhortation. It is at these moments I know to be silent and listen, because someone wiser and more experienced than me is speaking wisdom into my life.

He said, "You probably got here, to the admin building, about fifteen minutes early, didn't you?" To which I humbly nodded in affirmation.

"Well," he continued, "Why? Am I not only a man?"

It was becoming a little clearer but I still didn't know exactly where he was going with all of this.

He then proceeded to remind me of truths I had already learned, but somewhere along the way had lost sight of. Things like the simplicity of faith, and childlike eagerness to just "spend time with God." That if I showed up early all the time when meeting with mentors like himself—being mere men—how much more I should be eager to meet with God.

That specific word, on that particular day, really went straight to the heart for me. It is what brought me to realize that I had let slip from my mind and heart the great value of a simple faith. The importance of spending time alone with God had faded. More and more I felt as if I needed to "do" more in order to get closer to God. I had forgotten one of the most distinctive truths of the Christian faith, that which distinguishes it from all other religions, faiths and belief systems. I had lost sight of the most crucial element of salvation: that it is not a result of works.

In Memorandum

This reminds me that we are, all of us, forgetful people. We have heard and learned for years, centuries, and millennia, about the truth held out in the Bible: The stories of creation, the fall of man, and redemption through Christ. And yet, we still forget. Whether intentionally, or ignorantly, we lose sight of that which should be most important to us—that which is, and always has been, most important to our Maker: relationship.

God has made us with the intent of walking *with* us through life. His whole purpose for creating man was, and still is, relationship with His creation. He wants to *know* us and us to *know* Him, and, this not just in the sense that God knows everything. Yes, God is omniscient and knows more about each of us than we know about ourselves. But, He desires more than just knowing about us, He wants to *know* us, in personal constant contact. Likewise on the flip side of the coin: God wants us to *know* Him, not just know *about* Him.

This subject brings to mind the story about Israel—God's chosen people— wandering in the desert. For forty years they wandered around in circles through the desert waiting to enter the Promised Land. They wandered for forty years because they didn't hold on to and remember God's goodness to them. As soon as they faced hard times, they grumbled, complained and cursed the God who had miraculously rescued them from the evil hand of Pharaoh. As a matter of fact, their grumbling began only a few days after this supernatural deliverance.

> When Pharaoh's horses, chariots and horsemen went into the sea, the LORD brought the waters of the sea back over them, but the Israelites walked through the sea on dry ground… Then

> Moses led Israel from the Red Sea and they went into the Desert of Shur. For three days they traveled in the desert without finding water. When they came to Marah, they could not drink its water because it was bitter. (That is why the place is called Marah.) So the people *grumbled* against Moses, saying, "What are we to drink?"
>
> -Exodus 15:19, 22-24 (NIV; *italics mine*)

God let them wander because He knew that until they could be totally dependent on Him for everything they needed, and trust Him and love Him with all of their heart, they would not be ready to properly handle the destiny that awaited them. We, just like the Israelites, are forgetful people. We do not hold as tightly as we should to the memory of the wonderful works God has done in our lives.

You may be thinking to yourself, "God has never done any wonderful works in my life." And I would say that is because you have either forgotten what He has done for you, or you never even noticed. You see, God has always been around and active in the lives of people. He was there with Adam and Eve in Eden, and He is here with us now. He is with you when you rise in the morning and when you lay down at night. He never leaves you, but you can leave Him. Yet, even when we run from God, He does not leave us alone. He pursues us. He waits eagerly for the day we will choose to open up to His love and let Him guide the course of our life. King David said it most beautifully in one of his Psalms:

> You have searched me, LORD,
> and you know me.
> You know when I sit and when I rise;
> you perceive my thoughts from afar.
> You discern my going out and my lying down;
> you are familiar with all my ways.
> Before a word is on my tongue you,
> LORD, know it completely.
> You hem me in behind and before,
> and you lay your hand upon me.
> Such knowledge is too wonderful for me,
> too lofty for me to attain.
> Where can I go from your Spirit?
> Where can I flee from your presence?
> If I go up to the heavens, you are there;
> if I make my bed in the depths, you are
> there.
> If I rise on the wings of the dawn,

> if I settle on the far side of the sea, even
> there your hand will guide me, your
> right hand will hold me fast.
> If I say, "Surely the darkness will hide me and
> the light become night
> around me," even the darkness will not
> be dark to you; the night will shine like
> the day, for darkness is as light to you.
> -Psalm 139:1-12 (NIV)

In order to maintain a healthy relationship with God, we must always remember His constant presence in our lives. This is what the Israelites failed to do. They had forgotten that God was with them because they could not see Him with their mortal eyes. They only praised God when they tangibly saw His blessings poured out in their midst, yet as soon as the visible evidence of God's handiwork had vanished, their memory of it faded as well. They had a surface-level faith, one that was based solely on what God could *do for them*.

But God was not, and never will be, a genie in a lamp! He was asking for a faith based upon every-day-dependence on Him, with thankfulness for who *He was*, and not just what He was able to do. Bringing it a little closer to home, right here in modern day: how much this is like us. We only call on God when we need Him, when we're in trouble. We then go on living the rest of our lives as if He wasn't even real. Sure, we may even thank Him for His goodness to us when He helps us out of tough situations, but then just like the Israelites, we go back to our daily routine of faithlessness and complaining.

So what is it going to take for us to return to our original purpose of being in right relationship with God, our spirit united with His? How long must we postpone the blessings God has for us, the "Promised Land" He wants to give us? It is a choice that only we can make; God refuses to make it for us. What will we choose: constant wandering through life without a clue where we are going and why we're so lost? Or, will we do what the Israelites failed to do and force ourselves to recognize and remember the wonderful works of God in our lives? Let us return to a child-like faith in God, one that simply loves and trusts Him. A faith that is simply dependent on God for all we need and longs to spend quality time in His presence.

Constant Contact

The Bible tells us to "pray without ceasing." (1 Thes 5:17; NASB) What does this mean? Is it insinuating that one must recite prayers all day long? Not necessarily. What is ultimately being said here is that prayer and time spent alone with God is not based upon formula. How impossible it would be for you to continue saying memorized prayers all day long. For one thing, people would probably run away from you taking it that you had a few screws loose. Not to mention, you would never actually get anything done properly because you would be too distracted trying to remember all the words to your pre-rehearsed prayers.

No, God does not ask us to recite particular prayers over and over all day every day. Thank God! He knows how little skill *I* have with memorization! Even when we look at the famous Lord's Prayer, Jesus was not giving a particular formula or recitation for us to go through every day. He was simply giving us guidelines for our hearts and thoughts when we pray. It has always been His intent to be relational, and relationship requires a natural flow, not a stuffy religious practice.

> "This, then, is **how** you should pray:
> "'Our Father in heaven, hallowed be your name, your kingdom come, your will be done, on earth as it is in heaven. Give us today our daily bread. And forgive us our debts, as we also have forgiven our debtors. And lead us not into temptation, but deliver us from the evil one.
>
> -Matthew 6:9-13 (NIV; *emphasis mine*)

Notice this Scripture does not say, "This, then, is *what* you should pray…" Rather it clearly says, "This, then is *how* you should pray…" Jesus was giving an example of the *way* we should pray. He was giving us an outline of the important elements involved in sincere and reverent prayer. He was not, however, telling us to pray the same prayer every time we pray. The NKJV says it like this, "In this *manner*, therefore, pray…" And another translation puts it this way, "Pray *like* this…" (NLT)

If the crux of Christianity is relationship with God, why doesn't it look like such in the lives of more believers? Why do so many people have a misconception about what prayer actually is? Because too many allow it to become a mere religious act and practice instead of a natural free flowing relationship.

Just think about it. Would you say the same thing every single time you talked to your spouse, parents or brothers and sisters? What about your friends? Of course you wouldn't. They'd probably think you were off your rocker. Well, I wonder how God feels when we treat Him this way. We rarely ever spend time alone with Him, and even if we do take a few minutes out of every day, the rest of the day we give Him little thought or notice save the little prayer we may recite over dinner.

To pray without ceasing means a continual openness to communication with God. It's like a constant conversation. Think of it this way. Let's say you go shopping with a friend one day—both of you busy perusing different kinds of merchandise: clothing, movies, books, and so on. You might want to get your friend's opinion on things here and there.

"Hey, what do you think about this one? It looks pretty good."

"I don't know, maybe that other one is better."

This is a continual conversation. You are occupied with the things of life, but never cease communicating with those who share it with you. You keep the line open so that at any moment your friend wants to talk to you and vice versa, this is an instant possibility. But, this analogy comes nowhere close to describing relationship with God, does it? Because, as it is, there will be times when you cannot reach your friend to talk. There will be moments when even your own family is out of reach.

But God is available twenty-four-seven. It doesn't matter what time of the day, or night; we can call on Him. It doesn't matter where on earth we are because He is there too. He wants us to spend every day with Him, keeping that line of communication open so that at any moment He can speak to us. Or, if we have something on our heart to share with Him, we can do it in an instant. This is relationship. This is prayer. This is conversation with the Creator.

- CHAPTER FOUR -

NEO-GENESIS: A NEW BEGINNING

"Who can doubt that the world has undergone a kind of breakdown, the cosmic counterpart to a psychological breakdown in an individual. As a species we have lost a sense of self and of meaning, and we struggle to put life together in a coherent whole. A sly, chronic disease prevents us from relating to creation and each other, let alone God, as we should."

-Philip Yancey[8]

- Chapter Four -
Neo-Genesis: A New Beginning

It was a warm summer's evening in the year of two thousand and three. I had just spent the last couple of hours with the policemen who arrested me while I was trying to evade their capture of me. Even as rebellious and lawbreaking as I was at the time, I never made it a habit of running from police officers. It's not exactly the most intelligent thing to do. However, this particular night, I had on my person multiple bags of marijuana and was intoxicated. This was a night I really didn't want to get stopped by cops!

Little did I know, as I was frantically pushing the pedals on my bike, weaving through alleyways to escape, that this night would be one of the most significant moments of my entire life! There I was, hours later, kneeling on my bedroom floor next to my bed.

The policemen had, miraculously, allowed me to remain at my home for the night, instead of having to spend it in a cold jail cell. It was then I began to pray.

Oh, believe me, I had been praying in the back of that police car! Praying my heart out. But those prayers were merely, "God, if you get me out of this…" kind of prayers. No, it was after all of this that I found myself in connection with God like never before. As I knelt, I began to pray like I had never done. I prayed relationally. "God" I said as tears rolled off my face, "I surrender." "Jesus, I know I've tried to make something out of my life with my own hands and failed time and again! I give you all of me, every part of my life. Change my life. Change *me*."

Well, that is one powerful prayer to pray, to say the very least. There is nothing God loves more than when one of His lost children—anyone who isn't walking with Him—comes running into His arms with a surrendered heart. He began to change me that night, and He kept changing me! Matter of fact, He's *still* changing me, every single day.

But this is my story. You need a story of your own. You need to be able to say that God has changed your life and brought you freedom from sin. Wouldn't you love to know that you are in right relationship with the One who made you? And, don't you long to know that you will be in heaven when you die? Well, it begins with transformation. It starts by being "born again."

Salvation Prayer

Contrary to what some people might believe, "getting saved" is not just about "praying the prayer". It's not just this cute little moment of asking Jesus into your heart. It's a radical, earthshaking experience that will change the very course of your life. I'm sure there are a lot of people in the world who believe they are going to heaven when they die, and even dub themselves "Christians" simply because they "believe" in Jesus, or asked Him into their heart. This is simply not biblically sound.

Salvation is absolutely one hundred percent free, but that doesn't mean it's easy. It is by far the hardest thing in the world for a fallen human being to surrender their entire life to an unseen Being, especially when it means we get no credit for it. It most certainly wasn't easy for God to descend to earth, be confined to an earthly body and endure more suffering than anyone who's ever lived. But this is what He paid for us. He came to show us how bad sin looks, but in perfect contrast, how powerful His love is for us, and that He would stop at nothing to make free passage for us to be in relationship with Him.

With all of this in mind, don't you think it only fair for us to treat the issue of salvation with just a bit more reverence? Becoming a Christian is not just learning all the right phrases and prayers. It isn't having pictures of a blue eyed, blonde haired Jesus in your house or going to church every Sunday and Wednesday. To be a Christian means that you are to become more like Christ every day—to be constantly changed from the inside out. There is the initial change of course, when you realize you've been wrong and in sin all your life and thus repent, but there is also a continual change that we must be open to.

Red Pill, Blue Pill

In one of my favorite movies, *The Matrix*, there is a radical spiritual principle weaved throughout that excellently illustrates this topic. Thomas Anderson (aka Neo), the protagonist of the film, is faced with a great decision. Anderson has just been escorted by a group of mysterious people who tell him he will find what he's been looking for all these years: answers. He is led to an abandoned building where he is introduced to a man named Morpheus—a man who, up until this moment, was only legend to him; a man who Anderson had been searching for with intensity for a long time.

> "Take the blue pill, the story ends, you wake up in your bed and believe whatever you want to believe. Take the red pill, you stay in Wonderland, and I show you how deep the rabbit hole goes."[9]

This is the proposition Morpheus makes to Anderson as he holds out the red and blue colored pills in the palms of his hands, awaiting Anderson's decision. Anderson chooses the red pill of course, and the rest is history. He finds out that the world he's been living in is only an illusion created by machines; that mankind is in slavery to the machines aside from the elite few who were "set free" from such bondage, the Resistance if you will. He learns that the world behind the scenes—the real world—looks a whole lot different than the one that is simply a computer program: the Matrix. He also discovers that this "Matrix" world can be manipulated. As Morpheus tells him in one scene, "Some rules can be bent, others can be broken."

Morpheus in this way is challenging Anderson's so-called reality. In another scene—where he and Anderson have been doing hand-to-hand combat in a sparring computer program—Morpheus brings Anderson to a paradigm shift on reality. He says to Anderson, "If 'real' is what you can feel, taste and see, then real is simply electrical signals interpreted by your brain." This thought challenges our every day life. Do not we, as humans, live most of our hours, days, weeks and months this way, by natural impulse?

We get hungry, and so we eat. We get tired, and so we sleep. We feel lonely, and we pursue friends to spend time with. And we could go on and on about all the different 'feelings' of life that seem to guide our actions. But this is the challenge presented to us—to our thought processes. What if life is more than mere impulses? What if the truest reality is of a substance we cannot feel, smell, taste or see? Maybe that which is most real must be *pursued* in order to be discovered.

Morpheus held out to Mr. Anderson the choice to be awakened from his so-called reality—to be brought to the truth—or to remain in deception as if nothing ever happened. So it is with God: Jesus holds out to us, in His word, the choice to either accept truth and be changed so that we can be free and see the world as it really is, or remain in a false reality.

It is not enough to simply say, "I believe that Jesus exists." Anderson believed that Morpheus existed, but nothing changed in his life until he met him face to face, and accepted his proposition to be set free. Anderson knew he might not like what he saw when his eyes were opened to the truth. In fact, he was probably terrified of the possibilities. But, he chose the red pill. Not because it was the easy choice, or comfortable decision. He chose it because he wanted to know the truth, even if that truth didn't look pretty.

We are now faced with a choice of our own. The world we live in, our daily routine, the people we spend time with; none of it is as it seems at first glance. There is a substance, a mystery behind everything, but our eyes must be opened to see it. There must be a change in the way we think, a renewing of our minds as is put forth in the book of Romans:

> "Do not conform any longer to the pattern of this world, but be *transformed by the renewing of your mind.* Then you will be able to test and approve what God's will is—His good, pleasing and perfect will." -Romans 12:2 (NIV)

We will not be able to see things the way they really are, and more importantly, the way that they *should be*, without the initial *and* continual change that comes from salvation. We must either choose the red pill or the blue pill. There is no grey pill. There are no in-betweens. We are either on one side of the fence or the other. Oh what joy awaits those who choose the truth, but how those will be pitied who willfully remain in slavery and deception. For, the "happiness" of this world is over far too soon and there is nothing pleasant about what follows. Those who choose the truth will face many troubles in life but will have lasting joy and peace, and will enter into the greatest fulfillment of both. As is stated in the book of first John:

> "Do not love the world or anything in the world. If anyone loves the world, love for the Father is not in them. For everything in the world—the lust of the flesh, the lust of the eyes, and the pride of life—comes not from the Father but from the world. The world and its desires pass away, but whoever does the will of God *lives forever.*" -1 John 2:15-17 (NIV UK)

Another translation puts it this way:

> "Don't love the world's ways. Don't love the world's goods. Love of the world squeezes out love for the Father. Practically everything that goes on in the world—wanting your own way, wanting everything for yourself, wanting to appear important—has nothing to do with the Father. It just isolates you from him. The world and all its wanting, wanting, wanting is on the way out—but whoever does what God wants *is set for eternity*. (MSG)

RX Salvation

After taking a one-time dose of whatever was in that red pill, Mr. Anderson was never the same. He was awakened to reality as it is and never went back to the way things were. He was now alive in the truth and free from the bondage of deception that held him for his whole life. Now the question arises, could he lose his freedom? Could his life-change be reversed? This is a question extremely important to address, just as a few paragraphs back we discussed the "salvation prayer" and how salvation is a continual process and not just a one-time event.

Further on in the film, we are drawn to focus on another character: Cypher. This guy is shady to say the least. He is untrustworthy and really into himself. But, he is one of the freed. He too, like Anderson and the others, has been awakened to the truth. [In the context of our topic, he is a fellow Christian, if you will.] There is a scene where he is actually meeting with one of the enemies—a software program designed to eliminate threats to the Matrix—to discuss how he can be re-inserted into the Matrix—the fake, computerized dream world—in return for betraying Morpheus and the rest of the Resistance into the enemy's hands.

Just as in this fictional story, it is in fact possible for someone to give himself or herself back over to slavery after being set free. Cypher just wanted temporary pleasures, momentary satisfaction. He wanted to go back to sleep and keep dreaming that the world was this wonderful place that would provide for all his cravings. He was willing to sacrifice truth for a lie and it was more than possible for him to do as he wished. As Tolstoy once said, "Materialists mistake what limits life for life itself." This scenario brings to mind a very sobering section of Scripture.

> "And when people escape from the wickedness of the world by knowing our Lord and Savior Jesus Christ and then get tangled up and enslaved by sin again, they are worse off than before. It would be better if they had never known the way to righteousness than to know it and then reject the command they were given to live a holy life. They prove the truth of this proverb: "A dog returns to its vomit." And another says, "A washed pig returns to the mud."
>
> -2 Peter 2:20-22 (NLT)

Cypher, like Anderson, had at one time taken the red pill. Yet, with his own words in a conversation with Anderson, he sadly proclaimed, "Why oh why didn't I take the blue pill?" He had let an infectious attitude of selfish pleasure and his longing for carnal comfort overtake his thinking. Instead of allowing his mind to be continually renewed in the truth, it became corrupted and stagnate, dull, apathetic and unfaithful. The result? He ended up betraying his own kin and sacrificing his freedom, and eventually his life, for only himself. It was the most ignoble way to die.

Philip Yancey once said, "For many, sin feels like a kind of slavery—or in modern terms, an addiction. Any member of a twelve-step program can describe the process. Set a firm resolution against yielding to your addiction, and for a time you bask in freedom. How many though, experience the sad return to bondage."[10] And this is the story of Cypher. Though he was released from bondage and basked in that freedom for a time, he sadly returned to the pigpen of his own demise.

I realize I've done a great deal of exploring this fictional story, but I think it is a beautiful way of describing and pointing to a powerful biblical truth. And, even if the Wachowski brothers—the creators of the film—did not intend to communicate all that I have touched upon, the illustrations are in fact there, as you can clearly see. We may look at this story and say, "I would *never* do what Cypher did!" But, truth be told, if we allowed the earthly, carnal desires that are at work within our body to remain strong, they would eventually overtake us just as they did him.

Where it all Began

Since the fall of man, things are not as they should be. There is something rotten inside every person who enters the world that must be remedied. This rottenness is not very evident in the early stages of life, from birth to the toddler stage for instance. For when a child is too young to know the difference between right and wrong, are they not innocent and free from judgment of sin? But, this is somewhat of a probationary period so to speak, that comes to a close as soon as the child gains the ability to reason. For once he knows the difference between right and wrong, he is then accountable for his actions.

Nothing is purely evil in and of itself. Even the devil himself was once good, though now completely beyond any hope of redemption. But we will not delve into the details of that now. Angels are a far different thing entirely than humans, and God has held out redemption only for our kind, not for fallen angels. The devil is evil to the core and will always be that way, but we are not discussing the devil at present, rather, you and I. Mankind and the world itself is now plagued with an inherent corruption, but it wasn't always that way…

As C.S. Lewis once said,

> "Badness is only spoiled goodness. And there must be something good first before it can be spoiled."[11]

Once upon a time, as the true story goes, there was a man and a woman in a garden who walked with God. As a matter of fact they were in close fellowship with the Creator all day, every day. But something went wrong, terribly wrong. Man made a decision that cost every person thereafter their ultimate freedom and fellowship with God. This decision compromised the trust between the Creator and the created, and resulted in the corruption of the world. When Adam and Eve partook of the Fruit, a kind of poison entered their veins. It is a toxin that now flows within the bloodstream of all mankind, to which there is only one remedy: the Blood of Christ.

The tree that the first man and woman were ordered not to eat from was called the Tree of the Knowledge of Good and Evil. It is quite interesting to note that God did not tell them they would never receive the knowledge of good and evil. He simply told them not to eat from the tree. In essence, He was reassuring them that He wanted to be their sole source of wisdom and knowledge so that they wouldn't try to gain it on their own. This was really what the Fall was all about: man relying upon himself and denying God His rightful place as Teacher, Master, Shepherd and Father.

The way I see it is, God wanted to teach Adam and Eve everything they would need to know, but He would do this in His perfect timing. Much like an earthly father waits until the child progresses enough with understanding basic concepts to train him or her in more advanced ones. Another illustration would be the way in which a school system works. You cannot expect to understand trigonometry until you have mastered the basics of arithmetic. God knew that they would not be ready for the kind of information that the Tree offered, and thus commanded them not to pursue it on their own.

But now, post-Fall, we have a somewhat different dilemma. Every person *starts out* with a wrong way of thinking. And this we didn't have to choose; it is inherently in us. There is a malfunction in every human mind that must be repaired. Our thinking is automatically limited and misshapen. We are ultimately consumed with an attitude of self-seeking and neglect of God, as well as those around us. We naturally focus on the physical world and pay little, if any, heed to the supernatural realm. Spiritual concepts, even when somewhat understood remain foreign to us and we see no value in the investment of such "flights of fancy". We require a complete change of perspective, a challenge of the status quo in order to truly gain understanding into otherworldly truths.

It is like an unperceived prison. Much like the prison binding mankind that Morpheus reveals in The Matrix.

> "You are a slave Neo. Like everyone else, you were born into bondage, born into a prison that

> you cannot see, or smell, taste or touch. A
> prison for your mind."

Chris Seay and Greg Garrett in their book entitled *The Gospel Reloaded*, put it this way: "The journey to freedom cannot even begin until the captives begin to understand that they are held captive. But it isn't a question of stepping from enslavement to one sort of unalloyed freedom; it is stepping away from a debasing enslavement to a liberating one."[12] Truly, yielding oneself wholly to God ensues the greatest freedom.

And so, now we've come full circle. This is the exact position in which re-birth is most needed, when a person comes once again to the crux of existential purpose: being in right relationship with the *Creator of persons*. It is then and only then that the transformation begins. It is really in a sense a backwards evolution. For, in the beginning all things were "good" yet now the world is increasingly evil. If we continue living according to earthly thought and understanding, it only results in distancing ourselves even further from life, instead of advancing toward it.

- Chapter 5 -
Through the Fog

The fog of the fight,
Thick and unyielding.
From chaos and confusion
To cynicism and reclusion.
When all in me wants to hide,
To run from every battle left to fight
Let me stay, and be it necessary, slain
From day to day, suffering these losses
With the greatest joy; That in every death
I bear more the life and likeness of my Christ.
Guide me again my Good Father.
-Aaron Harper[13]

- CHAPTER 5 -
THROUGH THE FOG

We are now beginning to peel back the veil, the unknown becoming clearer. Yet, no matter how much knowledge and wisdom we acquire in this life, mystery will always remain. There is an overarching fog throughout all of life and there are seasons when the mist is thicker than usual.

What I have come to find in my own life, and which I hope you can also discover, is that this is not entirely a bad thing. As a matter of fact, it can, with enough effort and humility be seen as a tremendous blessing. After all, what fun would life be if we always knew everything that was going to happen? Where would the adventure be? Excitement and the joyful side of anticipation would cease to exist. As John Eldredge so excellently puts forth in his book *Wild at Heart*, "The most important aspect of any man's world—his relationship with his God and with the people in his life, his calling, the spiritual battles he'll face—every one of them is fraught with mystery. But this is not a bad thing; it is a joyful, rich part of reality and essential to our soul's thirst for adventure."[14]

Take a Flying Leap

A sailor drifting through a colossus of fog would never make the foolish attempt at wafting all the fog away so he could see clearer. Nor would he think it wise to jump up and down in a fit of rage yelling and screaming at the fog. No, trying to get rid of it or simply getting mad at it would not do. Neither would becoming depressed and laying down in defeat of it cause anything to change.

No, a wise sailor would know that his only resolution to this problem would be to hunker down and face the fog head on; to have his wits about him and utilize everything he's learned to navigate safely through it. He would need to have complete focus and attention to everything going on around him. And with all of these elements firmly intact, he would then be able to enjoy the mystery and adventure involved in this scenario. However, I think it would not be until after the fact that he could look back on this moment with appreciation when he had more relaxed time to reflect.

As we discussed above, there is a fog over our lives. We do not know what is going to happen today, tomorrow or the next day. We live in a constant state of mystery. Yes, we may make plans for today, and for our future, but the truth is, our plans can change. Life happens. Someone we love dies, we lose a job, a friend says they never want to see us again, we become ill. The list goes on and on of all the possible things that could happen to us in the course of a day, let alone a week, a month, a year.

We never know what's going to happen. So what do we do about this dilemma? As with the illustration of the sailor, it would do no good to become angry or depressed or try to blow the fog completely away. There is only one option left then; we must work through the fog. Live life in spite of it and never become discouraged just because we can't see everything clearly. And, in time, we may even learn to appreciate the fog.

Not Knowing Generates Faith

One thing that is really incredible about mysterious living is that it produces greater faith in God. The more we realize that there are things we don't know or understand about life, the more we come to grips with the fact that we don't run our own lives. And this gives birth to greater faith in God. It is only in the revelation of self-lack that our great need for divine help in every area of life is most evident. The mysterious nature of life actually draws us closer to God, if we allow it to, because we come to the conclusion that we cannot figure it out on our own.

> "Call to me and I will answer you. I'll tell you marvelous and wondrous things that you could never figure out on your own."
>
> –Jeremiah 33:3 (MSG)

We are in need of someone to guide us, to show us the way. Many times I wish that I would just know more about what's going to happen so that I could be more prepared for it. I often hope for things to happen a particular way, and when they don't, I have a choice to make; I can either become disgruntled, or roll with the punches and have faith that no matter what happens, God will see me through.

Step First, Then See

In the third installment of the Indiana Jones films, there is quite an inspiring scene. Jones is faced with multiple different obstacles on his quest to retrieve the Holy Grail, all having religious themes. My favorite one, however, is the "Leap of Faith."[15] Jones comes to the mouth of a seemingly unconquerable chasm with no way across to where the Grail is. He literally has to put his foot out and step on what appears to be only air. If this doesn't work, he will fall to his death hundreds of feet below.

Of course, if you've seen the movie you know what happens. Jones takes a large slow step and his foot meets solid ground. The camera then pans to the side and you see that there was a path all along bridging the gap, but it was disguised to blend in with the rock face on either side of the chasm. So from where he was standing, he was unable to see it with his naked eye.

Jones could have turned around and gone back at the sight of the chasm and the thought of falling to his doom, but he chose to have faith and take a step, and then, he saw. The concept of stepping before seeing is something dear to the heart of God, I believe. It is something that activates our faith like nothing else. We live in a world that always wants to "see it before they believe it." But, God comes to us to change that way of thinking. Requiring something to be shown to us before we can believe it does not demand much faith of us. Choosing to believe in something before we see it however, and acting upon that belief, requires from us great faith, and also builds great faith *within* us.

When Jesus called Peter out of the boat and onto the water, Peter did not have the privilege of seeing himself walk on water before he did it in some kind of vision. He didn't even get to see one of the other disciples do it first. If it was me in Peter's sandals, I might want to see my buddy try it first before I did! All he asked was that Jesus speak to him, and then he stepped. He walked on water. Wait; hold on, I don't think you got that. Let's say it together, HE WALKED ON WATER!

> Shortly before dawn Jesus went out to them, walking on the lake. When the disciples saw him walking on the lake, they were terrified. "It's a ghost," they said, and cried out in fear. But Jesus immediately said to them: "Take courage! It is I. Don't be afraid." "Lord, if it's

> you," Peter replied, "tell me to come to you on the water." "Come," he said. Then Peter got down out of the boat, walked on the water and came toward Jesus. But when he saw the wind, he was afraid and, beginning to sink, cried out, "Lord, save me!" Immediately Jesus reached out his hand and caught him. "You of little faith," he said, "why did you doubt?" And when they climbed into the boat, the wind died down. Then those who were in the boat worshiped him, saying, "Truly you are the Son of God."
>
> -Matthew 14:25-33 (NIV)

This is huge! Peter walked on water! I think far too often right after reviewing this part of the story we immediately think, "Well yes that's true, but then he started sinking." What's most important in this section of scripture is not that Peter started sinking, but that he actually stepped out. He didn't stay in the boat where he was most comfortable, he trusted God enough to walk to Him on water—liquid, H2O! Are you getting this? We sometimes think that we are facing the greatest challenges in the world, that no one has bigger obstacles. In response to this, I simply say, Peter walked on water.

Those Before Us

There are so many more stories in the Bible that portray the concept of "stepping before seeing" than just that of Peter walking on water. Interestingly enough, two of the stories that immediately come to mind also relate to water. After all, what else is more mysterious and unyielding to man than large, and violent, bodies of water?

The first story I would like to recall is that of Moses. I think you already know where I'm going with this one. I mean, who doesn't know about the parting of the Red Sea? Especially with the big-production animated motion picture, *Prince of Egypt* that came out some years ago. Or, for that matter, *The Ten Commandments*, which was released several years prior. So, even if you have never even read a Bible or been to church in your life, I think it safe to assume that you have heard of Moses and the parting of the Red Sea.

Nonetheless, even for those of us who have read the real account in Scripture numerous times and heard it preached just as much—if not more—on a Sunday morning service, this story speaks volumes to our faith, if we let it, regardless of how many times it has been relayed to us.

> Then the LORD said to Moses, "Why are you crying out to me? Tell the Israelites to move on. Raise your staff and stretch out your hand over the sea to divide the water so that the Israelites can go through the sea on dry ground"...Then Moses stretched out his hand over the sea, and all that night the LORD drove the sea back with a strong east wind and turned it into dry land. The waters were divided, and the Israelites went through the sea on dry ground, with a wall of water on their right and on their left.
>
> -Exodus 14:15-16; 21-22 (NIV)

It is interesting to note the first thing God says to Moses here, "Why are you crying out to me?" This would insinuate that is exactly what Moses is doing at the moment: crying out to God. It begs the question, are there times when we should simply be stepping out in faith instead of merely calling out to God to just show up in some miraculous way? Is it possible that God wants to work something miraculous through our simple act of stepping out and doing something? How often do we sit there crying out to God to do a miracle in our situation but don't take any steps to see Him move?

Upon God's command, Moses did just this. When He perceived that God was telling him to reach his staff out over the water and see what God would do, he did it. This may have appeared quite ridiculous to the Israelites. Who at this very moment were already grumbling about how they never should have left Egypt. They were afraid because an entourage of Pharaoh's angry warriors was headed at great speed toward them in that very moment. What would *you* think if you were one of the Israelites? "This guy Moses just promised us God's deliverance from slavery and now he's standing over an impassable body of water waving a stick around like an idiot!"

Moses did have something working to his advantage though, at least in the area of personal encouragement. He had already seen God work miracles by asking him to put forth his staff. Still, this was a miracle to trump all others! Parting a practically oceanic body of water so that all the Israelites could pass through on dry land before Pharaoh and his men could even reach them. And then, after arriving safely on the other side—every man, woman and child—God caused the sea to engulf their enemies behind them.

This was a miracle beyond anything Moses and the Israelites had ever seen. And it required a faith and trust in God—mainly on Moses' part—that was unprecedented. Here we see the "step-then-see" principle in action. It was time for Moses to not only pray, but move into action. He needed to activate his faith by stepping out, reaching the staff to touch the water, and then, he saw. And did he ever! Can you imagine what this must have been like? Two walls of water standing up on end like a couple of skyscrapers, and the ground between completely dry. And there the two giants stood, patiently waiting while thousands of people crossed through safely. It is incredible what God will do when people are willing to step out in faith before they see any tangible evidence.

Another story I would like to recall is that of Noah. Yes, another Bible story that you probably remember from Sunday school. This too is one of those biblical accounts that are so easy to breeze right through, simply because of the number of times we've heard reference to it. Or, merely the fact that we have this preconceived notion we already know everything we need to know about it—just like the story of Moses.

> "Noah was a righteous man, blameless among the people of his time, and he walked faithfully with God… Now the earth was corrupt in God's sight and was full of violence. God saw how corrupt the earth had become, for all the people on earth had corrupted their ways. So God said to Noah, 'I am going to put an end to all people, for the earth is filled with violence because of them. I am

surely going to destroy both them and the earth. So make yourself an ark of cypress wood; make rooms in it and coat it with pitch inside and out. This is how you are to build it: The ark is to be three hundred cubits long, fifty cubits wide and thirty cubits high. Make a roof for it, leaving below the roof an opening one cubit high all around. Put a door in the side of the ark and make lower, middle and upper decks. I am going to bring floodwaters on the earth to destroy all life under the heavens, every creature that has the breath of life in it. Everything on earth will perish. But I will establish my covenant with you, and you will enter the ark—you and your sons and your wife and your sons' wives with you. You are to bring into the ark two of all living creatures, male and female, to keep them alive with you. Two of every kind of bird, of every kind of animal and of every kind of creature that moves along the ground will come to you to be kept alive. You are to take every kind of food that is to be eaten and store it away as food for you and for them.'

Noah did everything just as God commanded him."

-Genesis 6:9-22 (NIV; *spacing emphasis mine*)

Let's take a look at the scenario here for a moment, set the stage. God tells Noah that He is going to destroy all living things on the face of the earth, except him and his family, so long as he actually builds the Ark and he and his family get in it. Then He gives specific instructions for how He wants this Ark to be built. And then He tells Noah to collect every kind of food there is, as well as two of every animal to bring into the Ark with them.

God comes to Noah with a pretty heavy word. Wouldn't you start becoming a little emotional if God told you He was about to completely wipe out everyone on the earth except for you and your family? But, God doesn't stop there. He doesn't just tell Noah what *He* is going to do, He then proceeds to ask *Noah* to do something: to take a flying leap of faith into the unknown.

In order to properly understand the velocity of God's request upon Noah, we must realize the details of the state of the world when He spoke it. According to some very likely interpretations of Scripture, rain had not yet been seen by anyone on earth because it was watered by mist coming up from the ground (Genesis 2:6). And if this is true, we can see that Noah must have had a difficult time wrapping his mind around it. It required great faith from him. And not only faith to believe that God would cause water to fall from the sky—for the first time in the history of the world—but also a faith to follow through with what God was asking him to do even when all around him would mock and scoff at the absurdity of it.

You see, not only did God speak a word to him about what *He* was going to do; He was preparing *Noah* to act upon this word. Like with Moses, God was saying this is not the time to be sitting around praying for Him to move but acting out upon the word He had already spoken. The people in Noah's day had never seen rain before. And they most certainly would have looked with spite upon Noah as he built a large floating vessel nowhere near any water. And to top it all off, this was an enormous structure!

> "According to the description, the ark was not a ship, but an immense house in form and structure like the houses in the East, designed not to sail, but only to float. Assuming the cubit to be 21.888 inches, the ark would be five hundred forty-seven feet long, ninety-one feet two inches wide, and forty-seven feet two inches high."[16]

This was an incredible obstacle that Noah was facing. Now, we don't really know what profession Noah was in, but I'm pretty sure he wasn't very versed on the art of Ark-making. No one had ever seen, or heard of, anything like this before. And even though God gave specific instructions for how He wanted it built, it wasn't a task that Noah could simply set out on by himself. He needed God's guidance, provision and protection through the whole process. And can you imagine how difficult it would be to round up two of every living thing on planet earth, as well as every kind of food? God literally was going to recreate a new earth through His faithful servant Noah. How would you feel in his shoes? Terrified? Fulfilled? Maybe both. But this story of faith does us no lasting good unless we take its truths and apply them to our own lives. We must jump into the story and allow ourselves to become part of it. And in so doing, we discover ourselves in it already. Bringing this a little closer to home let me give a personal life example.

Just the other day, I was brought yet again face to face with one of the greatest fogs in my life: finances. A merry-go-round of sorts it has been, always coming to a place of lacking monetary wealth. I'll be completely honest with you; my response to these frustrating moments is not always the most composed. As a matter of fact, it is almost completely undignified at times. Usually, upon realizing yet again that I have barely enough to pay the bills, there is a wave of depression that begins to overtake me. I feel inadequate, sad and even paralyzed. I think this struggle is greater for men, as we are wired to be providers, but I'm sure that women can also greatly relate to what I am saying now.

What comes next is the determining factor, however. At this point I am faced with a decision. I can either surrender myself to these feelings of depression and a victimized "giving up" mentality, or I can throw a fit of rage, *or* I can make the most difficult decision of all and praise God in the midst of it, trusting that He will get me through it and taking the necessary steps to act upon that declaration of faith. I know, this sounds ridiculous, and just doesn't really match up with common sense. Why would you praise God for something that is killing you inside? Why would you thank Him for allowing you to experience such grief and pain? How could you bring yourself to actually appreciate what you are going through?

I will not lie to you and tell you that this is an easy thing to do. Every time I'm faced with struggles like these, I have to force myself to trust in God. But it takes more than just positive thinking; it requires also calling to remembrance what He has done in the past. Just like what we discussed in chapter three, we are forgetful people, and as such it is difficult at times to simply remember that God has gotten us through tough situations before. There is power in this exercise of recollection.

Whenever we face our seemingly unconquerable wall of adversity as we pursue what God has called us to, it is essential that we declare to ourselves, and others, what miracles God has already done in our lives. Recognizing the tangible evidence of past victories will fill us with hope and faith. The dark cloud shrouding our *view* may not be lifted, but at least the one *weighing us down* will be.

But maybe you are someone who has never really experienced a tangible miracle that you can recall. If this is the case, maybe now is the time. Just because it hasn't happened yet, doesn't mean it can't. Maybe now is the time for you to experience a miracle that one day will be the very memory which will get you through a future obstacle. And, as is the subject we've been discussing, we mustn't forget that the stories of those men and women of faith all throughout the Bible are some of our most powerful faith memories. Even though we aren't the ones in the actual story, by recalling the faith of others, we can be strengthened in our own.

Just recently, the following Scripture was quickened to me that directly correlates to my ongoing struggle with finances. It brought me great encouragement and strengthened my faith perspective. May it do the same for you.

> The wife of a man from the company of the prophets cried out to Elisha, "Your servant my husband is dead, and you know that he revered the LORD. But now his creditor is coming to take my two boys as his slaves." Elisha replied to her, "How can I help you? Tell me, what do you have in your house?" "Your servant has nothing there at all," she said, "except a small jar of olive oil." Elisha said, "Go around and ask all your neighbors for empty jars. Don't ask for just a few. Then go inside and shut the door behind you and your sons. Pour oil into all the jars, and as each is filled, put it to one side." She left him and shut the door behind her and her sons. They brought the jars to her and she kept pouring. When all the jars were full, she said to her son, "Bring me another one." But he replied, "There is not a jar left." Then the oil stopped flowing. She went and told the man of God, and he said, "Go, sell the oil and pay your debts. You and your sons can live on what is left."
>
> 2 Kings 4:1-7 (NIV)

When Elisha asks her, "What do you have in your house?" She replies, "Your servant has nothing there at all … *except a small jar of olive oil.*" I find it interesting that this sounds just like a story in the New Testament, when Jesus asked the disciples to feed the five thousand with only a few fish and loaves of bread. It seems God has a way of taking what we think to be only a little—or even, nothing at all—and doing great things with it.

Are you now facing an obstacle like Noah, Moses, Peter, the Widow, and yes, even Indiana Jones, that seems insurmountable? Maybe you feel called to something that is far bigger than anything you are capable of. You have a slight vision of something in the future but have no idea how to see it through, and there it is before you, wrapped in so much mystery.

I believe that as we call to remembrance the stories of those who've gone before us and even find ourselves in their stories, we can be encouraged to let God write a new story with our lives today. What is your "Ark"? What is your "Red Sea", your crashing waves, or impassable chasm? Instead of getting angry, giving up or trying to eliminate the fog that veils our vision, may we press through what is unseen with faith like those of old. May we take the "little" we have, like the Widow, and believe that in God's hands, it can become much. And maybe, just maybe, we will actually learn to appreciate the great mist that keeps us in suspense.

"I will take the Ring," he said,

"Though I do not know the way."

-The *Fellowship of the Ring*, J.R.R. Tolkien[17]

- Chapter 6 -

The Anonymous Killer

"We can identify some villains, to be sure: suicide bombers who target civilians, priests who abuse children, drug lords in Latin America. The problem is, evil rarely announces itself so brazenly. Like citizens of an industrial city who no longer notice the pollution, we cannot detect more subtle evils in our cultural atmosphere. We live in a modern world so disordered from the original design that the entire notion of what is good for us has turned upside down."

-Philip Yancey[18]

- Chapter 6 -

The Anonymous Killer

There I lay, body quivering in a cold sweat, unable to speak because I could barely breathe. I had been suddenly awakened in the middle of the night with my hands perfectly at my sides underneath my blankets, which were now tightly pressed against my throat. As I lay there gasping for air and half coherent, I wondered if what I was experiencing was real, or if it were merely one of those frustrating "dream within a dream" moments. You know, the ones where you wake up inside of your dream completely believing that you are awake, then suddenly it dawns on you that something isn't right and you are still dreaming.

After a few brief seconds, which seemed like an eternity, it was more than clear that this was actually happening. I couldn't breathe; my own blankets were strangling me! Remember, as I just said a moment ago, my hands were underneath the covers, arms extended perfectly alongside my body. There is no way I could have been choking myself by pulling on the blankets. I played this over and over in my head and know for a fact that this is what was actually happening.

Having been raised by Christian parents, I knew what I was supposed to do in these situations. My mother taught me when I was very young that when I had really bad dreams and such I should simply call on God for help. She taught me that the name of Jesus was very powerful when called upon with sincerity, and so, I did just that. I began the attempt of calling upon the name of Jesus for help, but the words would barely come out. I was actually being suffocated and could barely breathe! I was terrified! So I tried even harder, "J…Je…JE..SU….S! JESUS!!" I finally shouted out.

Suddenly, with that cry of childlike desperation for my Savior to rescue me, the grip around my neck was being loosed and I could actually see—though vague in the dark and a dazed half-sleep—the outline of an enormous winged shadow crouched upon me with large dark hands slowly releasing my throat. The wingspan of this creature filled my entire room. I realized at that moment that it was not my blankets strangling me but this thing that was on top of me. Then in an instant, a large glowing arm just above this creature quickly grabbed the shadow by the neck and pulled it off of me with a jolt. It was gone, in an instant. There was then a peace and overwhelming feeling of safety that filled my room. I could tangibly feel the presence of God and knew that I was protected.

True Story

The story I just told is completely true, and I have relayed it in detail to the best of my memory. It occurred a very short time after I had committed my life to Christ and left a lifestyle of worldliness behind me. It is my earnest belief that there was a demonic force attempting to take my life because I had gone from the Kingdom of Darkness to the Kingdom of Light (more on Kingdom talk later).

I share this story for three reasons. First, I share it to show the velocity of hate the enemy of your soul—Satan—has toward you, and how that hate is seen much more tangibly when one becomes a Christ-follower. After all, why would the enemy feel the need to fight against you if you were part of his own kingdom?

Secondly, I share it to balance the darkness in proportion to the light, and that it pales in comparison. Darkness must run from light; it has no other choice. Lastly, I share this story to bring attention to the fact that there are forces of darkness that exist and have a much greater effect upon our lives than we perceive.

The Marionette Syndrome

Contrary to what many believe, the decisions we make in life are not solely dependent upon ourselves. What I mean is that there are influences to our decisions outside of ourselves, and more so than merely the circumstances we are in. In a sense, someone else is pulling our strings. This is true whether we like it or not. Yes, we make our own decisions, but the reasons we make those decisions are sometimes greatly influenced by unseen forces—whether good, or bad.

This thought brings to mind the film Pinocchio.[19] Though a children's flick, it actually bears much profound truth. As the story goes, Geppetto (a toymaker) desperately wants a son. He catches a glimpse of a shooting star one night, makes a wish on it—hence the famous "When You Wish Upon a Star" song—and a fairy appears who makes one of Geppetto's marionettes come to life. Geppetto names him Pinocchio.

At first, things seem to be going pretty well. Pinocchio is off to his first day of school and has his little cricket friend (conscience) to keep him out of trouble. In no time at all, however, he runs into some shady characters that realize the potential monetary gain involved with a living puppet and is steered—despite his helpful cricket—down the wrong path. Things proceed downhill pretty rapidly from here.

Pinocchio is then introduced to a man named Stromboli who makes him believe he is a friend to Pinocchio. Stromboli immediately puts Pinocchio on stage and has him sing the famous song, "I've Got No Strings." Ironically enough, bearing the given lyrics, in the next scene we see Stromboli forcing poor Pinocchio into a cage. He was deceived by this worldly man into thinking he was free to "live the good life" and do as he pleased; the somber reality being that he was actually a slave. He had unwittingly surrendered himself to a force that desired only harm for him.

Pinocchio's troubles don't end here however. Though he briefly escapes with help from his cricket friend and the fairy that brought him to life, he is immediately distracted and deceived by two other worldly men, Honest John and Gideon. These guys now tell him that he needs to go with them to a place called Pleasure Island. Pinocchio is convinced and goes with them. In their caravan to the island are many other young boys, one of whom Pinocchio befriends named Lampwick.

When on the island, Pinocchio and his newfound "friend" Lampwick indulge in careless living to its prime: choking back on cigars, tossing down pints and playing billiards in the world's biggest carnival. Though Pinocchio and Lampwick are having the time of their lives—or so they have been deceived to think—Pinocchio's cricket shows up and reveals the truth about this island. The discovery is made that the men who brought all the boys to the island had all along the devious plan of turning the boys into donkeys so they could be set to work as slaves for them.

By the time they realize this, however, it's too late; the transformation has already begun as the boys begin to sprout ears and tails like mules. Long-story-short, Pinocchio ends up escaping with help from his cricket and runs home, only to find that Geppetto has gone in search of him and isn't home. They end up searching in the ocean for Geppetto and are united with him in the belly of a giant whale named Monstro. They make the whale sneeze them out and escape into the sea. However, the whale makes an enormous tidal wave, which drowns Pinocchio. They take the lifeless doll home and mourn over him; the fairy then reappears and transforms Pinocchio into a one-hundred-percent real boy because he has proven himself brave and unselfish.

This story bears much light upon life as it really is. We often are enticed and directed by seemingly friendly forces in our lives toward things that we think will bring us fulfillment. After all, as we perceived in a previous chapter, there is an inherent malfunction in our own human nature since the Fall of Man, which naturally pulls us toward sinful desires.

Mouse in *The Matrix* said, "To deny our own impulses is to deny the very thing that makes us human."[20] This is the very deception that plagues us. Our "natural" impulses are no longer truly natural. For, the origin of what is natural precedes the Fall. Thus, what we think of as "natural" impulses and desires are in all actuality, very unnatural. Our true original nature is in a constant state of war with our deformed nature. But, this is something that can go unnoticed for an entire lifetime if left unchecked.

Being that we already have a corrupt inclination toward wickedness within our bodies, it is far easier than we realize to be drawn even further away from what should be our true nature—what God originally intended for us to be like. In order to be found in a true life of freedom and victory over evil, it is required of us to allow our eyes to be opened to the truth. We must realize that there are dark forces feeding upon the already sinister nature within us, dragging us toward greater evil than we would like to think ourselves capable of.

Who Are These Sick People?!

I recently came across a very disturbing story about a serial killer who dubbed himself the "crossbow cannibal."[21] The story hit UK newspapers back in December of 2010 of a man named Stephen Griffiths—a PhD student of homicide—who killed multiple women with a crossbow. Apparently, Griffiths lived in the red-light-district of Bradford, UK, and he lured the women—all prostitutes—into his flat there where he proceeded with the murders. According to newspapers, Griffiths claims to have also cooked and eaten parts of his victims.

According to one UK newspaper, when Griffiths was confronted with his charges, he said 'guilty' in a quiet voice and then sat with his head on his chest. I find this interesting due to the fact that in his previous confrontations with authorities, he was much more bold and blatant in his statements. Another UK newspaper stated that, according to authorities, "He has never said he regretted his actions or said in even the most perfunctory way he was sorry."[22]

Yet, this is not what I see in his response to being charged as guilty. You can almost sense that at least somewhere in his inner being he is being tormented by a true sense of guilt for what he's done—as if, deep down inside, he knew without a doubt what he did was wrong and he wishes he had never done it. This confusion within himself is further illustrated as we consider more evidence.

One night, during the events being discussed, Griffiths wrote on his MySpace social networking page under the unexplained pseudonym Ven Pariah, that he had "finally emerged into the world". The message continued as follows, "What will this pseudo-human do, one wonders. Poor Stephen, pretended to be me, but he was only the wrapping. He knew towards the end, that I supplied the inner core of iron. Hatred Bound Tightly In Flesh. At very long last, the time has come to act out."

This evidence serves as proof of something more than meets the eye. Griffiths is a man at war within himself, and the words proceeding from his own mouth seem to exhibit dual identities, as if it were not he speaking at times, but rather, someone else. This comes as no surprise to me, as I am fully aware of how forces of darkness can infiltrate someone who is not a true believer and actually make a dwelling within him. This in turn causes a tug-of-war, so to speak, between the real person and the demonic force manipulating the one being occupied by this evil. What results is almost a bi-polar effect, for lack of a better term. One minute it is obvious that Griffiths is speaking of his own accord, and the next it would appear that someone—or something—else is speaking for him.

Now, I am in no way trying to justify Griffith's gruesome and completely evil actions. We discussed man's tendency toward sinfulness in his own skin earlier. What I am trying to say here, however, is that his actions were highly influenced by unseen forces. It is my belief, that a powerful force of evil was possessing him and feeding upon the already corrupt nature within him, leading him to do unspeakable things. The strings pulling him like a marionette may be invisible to the naked eye, but upon closer inspection, we find he is a slave to an enemy whose only intention is to take his life and the lives of others. An anonymous killer if you will.

In reviewing this macabre and gruesome account, I am sure you could think of countless other stories equally disturbing. Jeffrey Dahmer, Charles Manson, Ted Bundy, Eric Harris and Dylan Klebold of the Columbine massacre, Hitler, even Jack the Ripper who committed gruesome murders back in 1888—which ironically also involved prostitutes. And there are countless others that could be mentioned, but it is not my intent to further add fame to any of their names. I simply mention them to more completely solidify the message being conveyed.

Pitchfork and a Pointy Tail?

We do not know what Satan looks like. But I think it quite safe to declare he does not look like what our paintings and comic strips portray him as: all crimson, pitchfork in hand, long pointy tail and a sinister pointed goatee. As a matter of fact, the Bible says that he, "masquerades as an angel of light." (2 Corinthians 11:14; NIV) Thus, the devil does not always surface as a terrible and macabre entity, but rather with an appearance that is appealing, enticing, even strangely attractive to our carnality.

After all, if the enemy of our souls revealed himself to us in a full frontal attack of pure evil, would we not surely turn and run for our very lives? Why then are so many trapped in his snares? Well, the Bible does also call him the deceiver. And someone who is deceived is unaware of what is truly happening to him. It's like the story of Pinocchio, who sings "I've got no strings on me!" While in all actuality he is dangling from the invisible strings of the evil puppeteer. He thought he was free as a bird in his new "adventure" with his new "friends." But the truth is he was trapped, held captive by invisible chords, tugging and pulling his will this way and that. Later however, the bars of his prison cell could be seen quite clearly. And the deformity, which resulted from surrendering himself to the false promise of worldly prosperity, was impossible not to notice. You can't get much more obvious than turning into a mule.

Full Circle

There are forces [of evil] at work here beyond what eye can see. And though the influence of such invisible powers may never bring us anywhere near the same corruption—and even "possession"—as those like the "Crossbow Cannibal," it is vital that we recognize the influence these forces have upon all of us, and find out how we are to battle them.

The mere awareness that there is an utterly evil being out there with minions of fallen angels at his disposal, should put us on guard with every ounce of our being. We should be even more careful to not open our hearts and lives to such destructive powers.

In the case of the "Crossbow Cannibal", and other gruesome cases throughout history, we see an interesting situation. We wonder why, if the devil comes disguised as an "angel of light" the situation looks so blatantly evil. It doesn't seem like the devil was trying very hard to hide. Well, I'm sure that the evil one didn't come to Griffiths in the appearance of absolute evil. Nor, was this the case with all the other murderers I've mentioned.

Quite the contrary, I think the devil appeared to these people in subtle, tempting ways, which appealed to their own carnal curiosity and emotions. So, even though to us, these appear to be blatant examples of satanic influence—"pitchfork and pointy tail"—this is not the way in which the offenders would have seen it. Oh yes, they may have seen the influence of evil in their life quite clearly and even recognized it as such, but it came to them at first as appealing.

Take for example Stephen Griffiths, who was a student of criminology and was obsessed with serial killers. Police said they found a surplus of literature in his flat about mass murderers. Griffiths surrendered himself to the demonic influence of these people's lives. And the result was a slow-progressive mutation of his own mind creating perfect opportunity for him to commit such evil with seemingly no remorse. In these gruesome headlines about murderers such as Griffiths, we see the effects of the "anonymous killer" go far beyond that of the victims, however, for the first victim was actually the killer himself. Again, in no way can their actions be excused. In my opinion they completely deserve the punishment ensued, and then some! But, nonetheless it cannot be denied that they made themselves victim—even if in subtle ignorance—to demonic forces more powerful than just their own sinful nature and capabilities for evil deeds.

So, in essence, in these stories everyone is a victim. Yes, the killer did terrible, unthinkable things. But the truth is, be it rather discomforting, we all—given the prime set of circumstances and continual subtle surrender to forces of evil—are capable of the same awful things, and worse. Even if these deeds are only done intentionally in the mind and heart of a person without ever been acted out physically.

Jesus did say that, "Anyone who hates his brother is a murderer, and you know that no murderer has eternal life in him." (1 John 3:15; NIV) Those are some harsh words, but unavoidable truth. Harboring hate in our heart and mind for another is just as bad as murder in God's eyes. Ever notice how easy it is to think violent, even murderous, thoughts about someone when we are truly allowing ourselves to be hateful toward them? We would never think ourselves capable of acting these thoughts out, but we mustn't be deceived; remember what happened to Stephen Griffiths. It's time for us to recognize our unseen enemy—to reveal the anonymous killer.

- Chapter 7 -

The Anonymous Killer II:

Knowing is Half the Battle

"Submit therefore to God.

Resist the devil and he will flee from you."

-James 4:7 (NASB)

- Chapter 7 -

The Anonymous Killer II: Knowing is Half the Battle

It is not enough to know that we have an enemy. It is not sufficient even to know what he is up to. There must also come an active resistance to the darkness that tries taking our lives for itself. But, one would ask, how is it possible to resist an enemy that cannot be seen? James tells us this is done by submitting to an Ally who is [also] unseen. "Submit therefore to God…" (James 4:7; NASB) We must come to grips with the fact that there is a realm unseen to the naked eye of humankind. A realm which, although in rare moments can be seen in glimpses, can only be *dealt* with by way of those who are already unseen.

What I mean is simply this, we cannot resist on our own terms. God and His angels know the devil and how he works far better than we ever could. The devil was, after all, previously an angel of heaven. God created him, just like all the other angels. And God kicked him out of heaven like a rebellious teenager. But, we wouldn't know any of this if we weren't approaching our enemy on God's terms—by listening to His voice, His word, as our primary source of information and guidance.

The only way to resist the devil and actually see him tuck tail and run (pardon my pun), is by submitting to God [first], trusting that He will send angelic protection reinforcing our resistance. His authority alone is enough to make the enemy run scared, but in order to truly walk in the authority of God over the devil, we must submit to God's authority. It sounds so simple, yet is very difficult for us to do.

The same rebellious pride, which rose in the heart of Lucifer—as he was formerly called in his heavenly days—is within every one of us. Like an infection coursing through our veins, our blood is polluted by the potential for unspeakable evil, and all beginning with simple pride. In Lucifer, this sin of pride was self-created, as he was a perfect being—like all God's creations—in the beginning. Though somewhat cryptic, we do have evidence of this story in scripture. Take the following to Scriptures for example:

The Anonymous Killer II: Knowing Is Half the Battle

"How you have fallen from heaven, O Star of the Morning (Lucifer), son of Dawn! You have been cut down to the earth, you who have weakened the nations!"

–Isaiah 14:12 (NASB; *parentheses Mine*)

"'You were the seal of perfection, full of wisdom and perfect in beauty. You were in Eden, the garden of God; every precious stone adorned you: carnelian, chrysolite and emerald, topaz, onyx and jasper, lapis lazuli, turquoise and beryl. Your settings and mountings were made of gold; on the day you were created they were prepared. You were anointed as a guardian cherub, for so I ordained you. You were on the holy mount of God; you walked among the fiery stones. You were blameless in your ways from the day you were created till wickedness was found in you. Through your widespread trade you were filled with violence, and you sinned. So I drove you in disgrace from the mount of God, and I expelled you, guardian cherub, from among the fiery stones. **Your heart became proud on account of your beauty**, and you corrupted your wisdom because of your splendor. So I threw you to the earth; I made a

> spectacle of you before kings. By your many sins and
> dishonest trade you have desecrated your sanctuaries. So
> I made a fire come out from you, and it consumed
> you, and I reduced you to ashes on the ground in the
> sight of all who were watching. All the nations who knew
> you are appalled at you; you have come to a horrible
> end and will be no more.'"
>
> -Ezekiel 28:12-19 (NIV; *emphasis mine*)

If that which caused Satan to fall from righteousness was pride—literally a "god-complex"—then it is obvious what the opposite is, humility before God. This only further validates the power that comes from humbling oneself before God, the key, as James says, to getting the devil away from you.

In other words, the remedy for the infection of pride within every human being is the humility that comes only from God. Again, this battle against evil cannot be fought in the natural; mere human understanding and strength cannot win it. We must beseech the One who has the ultimate authority over this invisible realm and play by His rules. The devil thought he could make up his own game plan, and we see where that landed him.

The God-Complex

Lucifer was the original sinner. His sin was not merely a small dose of pride. It may have started that way, but the thing about pride, as with all sin, is that it grows. Like a parasite, it is not satisfied with only a little, nibbling just enough and then leaving the victim alone. No, it feasts without ceasing when left unchecked and therefore leads to unlimited evil.

The most frightening thing about pride is that, as stated earlier, it is something already inside of each one of us. Again, with Lucifer, he was the first—the "pride protagonist" if you will—and his sinful nature was self-created. By spoiling his own goodness, he became rotten. But now, after man gave in to this original sinner's enticement, he invited in an infection now inherent to every person born into the world. We have this in us whether we like it or not.

Pride grows. It is not satisfied with little, it keeps sapping us of goodness until there is no more left. With Lucifer it grew to the point that he actually wanted to be glorified above God Himself. He wasn't satisfied with just being beautiful and powerful anymore. He began to desire God's very role, a futile and foolish desire that will never pan out well.

And this, the plight of Satan, is seen revealed in mankind. Just look again at the stories from the last chapter of the murderers we discussed. Especially with "The Crossbow Cannibal" and Jack the Ripper, who murdered prostitutes. It is almost as if these psychopaths thought they were doing the world a service by ridding it of "trash." Just look at the gruesome nature of the Ripper's killings. He actually completely removed the victims' reproductive parts,[23] almost as if to play God and take away that part of them that they used as agents of corruption.

These sinister acts reveal more than meets the eye. They bring to focus the reality of the first sin—committed by Satan, not man—being played out again and again in the lives of those who do not yield themselves to God and thus by default end up slaves of the devil himself. But, this god-complex does not come to fruition only in psychopaths and serial killers.

My mind is now drawn to think about the religious leaders of Jesus' days on earth. They, like Satan himself, had a god-complex. This only stands to reason as Jesus Himself called them out as "Children of the devil."

> "Jesus said to them, 'If God were your Father, you would love me, for I have come here from God. I have not come

> on my own; God sent me. Why is my language not clear to you? Because you are unable to hear what I say. *You belong to your father, the devil,* and you want to carry out your father's desires. He was a murderer from the beginning, not holding to the truth, for there is no truth in him.'"
>
> -John 8:42-44 (NIV; *italics mine*)

Like the murderers we discussed last chapter, the religious leaders Jesus addresses in this passage liked to play God. They made it a regular occurrence to overstep what God had actually commanded, overlooking the most crucial elements of God's word in order to reinforce their own agenda. Their pride was left unchecked and unchanged to the point that they simply followed suit with the original sinner, their true "father" as Jesus put it—the devil himself.

These leaders, like our murder subjects, were deceived by an "angel of light." They actually thought they were doing a service to the world, and to God, by their ridiculously legalistic actions. But, Jesus revealed their true motives, and the one by whom they were actually being influenced: the anonymous killer. We see the contrast between God's true character and that of the religious leaders in scripture. Take the example of the woman they caught in an act of adultery for instance. They brought her before Jesus and wanted to stone her to death for her heinous crime. They wanted to take matters into their own hands and cleanse the world from this sinner. Jesus, in complete contrast, challenged their deceptive reasoning and portrayed God's true character.

> "At dawn he appeared again in the temple courts, where all the people gathered around him, and he sat down to teach them. The teachers of the law and the Pharisees brought in a woman caught in adultery. They made her stand before the group and said to Jesus, 'Teacher, this woman was caught in the act of adultery. In the Law Moses commanded us to stone such women. Now what do you say?' They were using this question as a trap, in order to have a basis for accusing him. But Jesus bent down and started to write on the ground with his finger. When they kept on questioning him, he straightened up and said to them, 'Let any one of you who is without sin be the first to throw a stone at her.' Again he stooped down and wrote on the ground. At this, those who heard began to go away one at a time, the older ones first, until only Jesus was left, with the woman still standing there. Jesus straightened up and

> asked her, '*Woman, where are they? Has no one condemned you?*' 'No one, sir,' she said. '*Then neither do I condemn you,*' *Jesus declared.* '*Go now and leave your life of sin.*'
>
> -John 8:2-11 (NIV; *italics mine*)

What we see in this passage is God's loving compassion displayed. Jesus—God Himself in the flesh—submitted to God and resisted the devil. The result: all the accusers left, one by one. Jesus displays for us what truly humbling oneself before God and resisting the devil looks like.

If the religious leaders had had their way, they would have taken the life of this woman into their own hands, just like serial killers obsessed with ridding the world of prostitutes. Thus we see that the overly religious and psychopathic killers shockingly share something in common, both groups of people like to play God. This further illustrates the depth at which the enemy infiltrates people's lives. But, because he operates mainly in the unseen realm, how can we hope to know the truth without proper illumination from the One who sees all?

Wielding the Word

If resisting the devil comes by humbling ourselves before God, and humbling ourselves requires living on God's terms, we must understand what God's terms are, and the only way to know that is by having a firm grasp on what the Word of God says—for it is in His Word that we find His "terms."

Jesus again perfectly displayed what this looks like for us—in Matthew chapter four, verses one through eleven—when He was led by the Spirit of God into the wilderness to be tempted by the devil. When the devil came to tempt Him, it is interesting to note that he didn't come at him with a full frontal attack. Remember, he comes in disguise with deceptive enticement. His method didn't change, even for Jesus Himself.

The deceiver actually came at Him with Scripture! He misused and took out of context different scriptural references in an attempt to get the Son of God to cave in. The thought that the devil, being the epitome of evil, would actually speak scripture to accomplish his devious plans—though out of context and proper application—should cause a greater urgency in us for more holistic scriptural understanding.

This is how Jesus resisted the devil in the wilderness. He shut down the devil's attacks by revealing the truth of scripture, bringing to light the deceptive way that Satan was abusing the Word of God. Jesus, unlike Satan, rightly spoke the Word and that was His weapon of choice. Now, if Jesus Himself chose the Word of God as His weapon against the devil, who are we—people subject to His authority whether we like it or not—to think we can win against our foe any other way?

Skillful Blade

Getting spiritual understanding and knowledge of the Word of God is not something that occurs overnight. In Ephesians 6:17, we are given a list of spiritual armor that God equips us with in our battle against Satan. The only article of this armor that is offensive—actually an attacking weapon—is the Word of God, which we are told is our Sword. Now, for the sake of greater visual understanding let me illustrate this a little.

I think of Samurai for instance. These men of warfare would not run into battle the minute they were bestowed with a sword. I remember segments from the film *The Last Samurai* where Tom Cruise gets into a wooden sword duel with a Samurai.[24] The scene is somewhat pitiful. He gets knocked down again and again, but because of his own pride, and self-superiority complex, he keeps getting back up, only to be beaten so badly he cannot rise again. He had no skill with the Samurai sword. He knew how to shoot a gun and even fight with an American military sword, but this was a different kind of fighting than he was accustomed to. He lacked the experience with this particular blade and fighting style necessary for victory.

As the film proceeds however, we see him training night and day to become skillful with the Japanese blade. But, this only comes through diligence: practice, practice and more practice. He takes many blows in the process but continues to persevere. Late nights and early mornings, he devotes himself to becoming a skillful swordsman. And eventually, he does just that. He gets so good in fact, that the Samurai actually welcome him as one of their own.

Jesus was a skillful swordsman. He picked up the Scriptures at a very early age and devoted Himself to understanding what God was communicating through them. The Bible says that when He was only a boy, He impressed the religious teachers—who were many years His senior in scriptural studies—with His extensive knowledge of the Word. (Luke 2:47) Jesus Himself, through whom the entire universe was created (John 1:3), spent time developing His skill with the Word as His weapon.

The difficulty we face is that our battle is not one that is obvious all the time. As illustrated last chapter and into this one, we have an unseen foe that tries his best to stay hidden from us in his devious tactics. Tries to appear in friendly form instead of as a blatant enemy. This only further proves why the Word of God is our greatest weapon against this slippery villain—it helps us recognize that there is more than meets the eye and aids us in understanding how to approach this subtle-though-supernatural influence.

Reading Rightly

Without the Word of God, and a proper understanding of it, we stand no chance against the power and deceptions of Satan. As a pastor friend of mine once said, "If you don't stand up for something, you will fall for anything." But, even if we stand up for what we think to be a solid truth and yet do not let it be judged rightly by the Word of God, it may be that we are actually building upon a faulty foundation of biblical understanding; that we are building on a foundation of sand. And then, when the wind, rain and waves of opposition come beating against us, we will crumble instead of standing strong, as we should.

> "'Therefore whoever hears these sayings of Mine, and does them, I will liken him to a wise man who built his house on the rock: and the rain descended, the floods came, and the winds blew and beat on that house; and it did not fall, for it was founded on the rock. But everyone who hears these sayings of Mine, and does not do them, will be like a foolish man who built his house on the sand: and the rain descended, the floods came, and the winds blew and beat on that house; and it fell. And great was its fall.' And so it was, when Jesus had ended these sayings, that the people were astonished at His teaching, for He taught them as one having authority, and not as the scribes."
>
> -Matthew 7:24-29 (NKJV)

But, it takes more than just an understanding of Scripture to fight the enemy. This warfare requires action. We must rightly read and understand what we are reading, but also, we must do what we know should be done. Indeed, much of our understanding of Scripture comes from the acting upon it.

This is an interesting situation. For often we want to fully understand before we step out, but if we always approach our battles this way, we will miss out on further understanding that can only come to us through the action. We move forward with the little understanding we already have, and that understanding grows. Not only does it grow, but also we develop a more solid inner strength at the same time. Then begins the steady progression: read, understand, act, understand; read, understand, act, understand—and so the cycle of growth continues.

The more we practice this process in our lives, the stronger we become to hold up our weapon—and keep holding it in the midst of battle—and the more skillful we become in swinging it at the enemy. The Word of God is heavy like a double-edged broadsword, and even when we do have the strength to hold it up, it takes a lot more than simply holding it to defeat the enemy. Just because I have a Bible in my home, does not at all mean I am ready to use it as a weapon. I must learn how to wield it; I must become skillful in battle, just like Jesus.

We mustn't forget we aren't alone in this fight. God did not leave us to try and muster our own strength and skill to the point of being ready for battle.

We do have a lot of practice to undergo, hours upon hours of grueling training to develop our skill, but we are not left to our own devices for accomplishment of this. Let's revisit—more fully this time—the spiritual arsenal described in the book of Ephesians.

> "Finally, be strong in the Lord and in his mighty power. Put on the full armor of God so that you can take your stand against the devil's schemes. For our struggle is not against flesh and blood, but against the rulers, against the authorities, against the powers of this dark world and against the spiritual forces of evil in the heavenly realms. Therefore put on the full armor of God, so that when the day of evil comes, you may be able to stand your ground, and after you have done everything, to stand. Stand firm then, with the belt of truth buckled round your waist, with the breastplate of righteousness in place, and with your feet fitted with the readiness that comes from the gospel of peace. In addition to all this, take up the shield

of faith, with which you can extinguish all the flaming arrows of the evil one. Take the helmet of salvation and *the sword **of the Spirit**, which is the word of God.*"

-Ephesians 6:10-17 (NIV UK; *italics and emphasis mine*)

It is interesting to note the last statement in this list of spiritual warfare equipment, "the sword OF THE SPIRIT, which is the WORD OF GOD." Here we see what we have been talking about in that it says the Word is the sword—our offensive weapon. But, there is another very vital thing to notice here. It says that our sword is "the sword of the Spirit."

Well, what does that mean? Is it our sword, or the Spirit's sword? Do we wield it, or does God the Spirit? These are all very good and valid questions to ask. The answer is, essentially, both. It is our sword and we have a responsibility, and a desperate need, to pick it up and fight. But, it is also the Spirit's sword in that He is the one to direct our swing. I understand this may be a little confusing; bear with me here.

As born-again believers, the Holy Spirit indwells us—He literally makes His dwelling inside of us. (1 Corinthians 3:16; NASB) He guides our decision-making, if we let Him. (John 16:13) He comforts us when we are weak (2 Corinthians 1:5; NASB), He puts words of hope and life and truth in our mouths when we know not how to speak. (Luke 12:11-12) It would only make sense then that He also helps us in battle.

This is extremely encouraging! Simply knowing that we are not alone speaks volumes of empowerment to our hearts. But the good news doesn't stop there; if we stay yielded to the Holy Spirit in every area of our lives, He will guide and direct us in developing both our understanding of and skill with the Scriptures as our weapon against the enemy. He provides us with both wisdom and strength that we don't naturally have. For this is not a natural war we are caught up in; it is supernatural and otherworldly.

> "For though we live in the world, we do not wage war as the world does. The weapons we fight with are not the weapons of the world. On the contrary, they have *divine power* to demolish strongholds."
>
> -2 Corinthians 10:3-4 (NIV; *italics mine*)

Just as we require God's divine help in recognizing our invisible adversary, we equally need His assistance when *engaging* in spiritual warfare. God the Spirit wields our weapon *through* us. Something we are incapable of doing on our own. Yet, once again, this does not negate our responsibility to train. The Holy Spirit was not sent to us so that we could have the luxury of sitting back with a bucket of popcorn while He fights our battles for us. That is not His purpose. He comes rather to take us through the training process—blood, sweat and tears—that we would be ready for anything.

With the Spirit of God Himself working supernatural strength and skill in and through us, we have nothing to fear. Nothing is above God, not even Satan. Remember, he too is merely a created being, though much different from us. With God Himself indwelling and working through us in battle, we are unstoppable. The enemy doesn't stand a chance.

- Chapter 8 -

Peculiar Twists

“Faithless is he who says farewell when the road darkens.”

-J.R.R. Tolkien

- Chapter 8 -

Peculiar Twists

A few years ago, while I was still attending Bible College, my everyday life was shaken up in an instant. I hadn't noticed anything unusual about the day upon rising from bed, nor when I put on my athletic apparel and began my drive to the local fitness center. It was a nice day as best I can remember—not too hot and not too cold. And the weather wasn't the only thing nice. Things had been going pretty well. Yes, I was still a broke college student, but God had been providing and I was making all my bills as well as achieving a good grade standing. I still had enough money to attend the gym after all—something I don't even have an allotment for in my budget at the time of writing this.

When I made it to the gym, I proceeded with my usual workout: cardio, and triceps or biceps depending on the day. Then, when I had felt accomplished and needed to get back to campus for further study and whatever else my schedule for the day held, I got into my car and began my return trip. What came next, I wouldn't have guessed would happen in a thousand years. Approaching the intersection nearest the parking lot of the gym, my mind, for whatever reason—weariness from studies, the lull that sometimes comes following a good exercise session, or any other worries and cares—was somewhat dull. My light turned green and I proceeded across the intersection, singing along with the music on my car stereo. Little did I know, my schedule for the day was about to be completely rearranged.

I can still see the scene in slow motion with clarity. Just in front of me on the opposite side of the intersection, there was a van waiting to turn left at the light, I was driving straight. At first I merely glanced at this van assuming the driver would obviously wait for me to pass straight through before continuing to turn. This however is not what happened. Half way across, I realized this large van turning directly toward me was not stopping at all—in fact, speeding up!

As soon as I knew that this other driver was not going to stop, I pushed down the gas as hard as I could, but to no avail.

SLAM! Before I knew what happened, this 1980's brown Ford Windstar plowed its nose right into the driver's side of my car. I fish tailed and came to an immediate halt on the side of the road, sitting in shock and silence. As I glanced back to get a better look at the vehicle that took me out, hoping the driver and passengers were okay, and also expecting them to exit their vehicle and check on me, the van backed up and then drove away.

Such a mixture of emotions crashed over me in that moment: anger, mixed with anxiety, fear, doubt, frustration, and sadness. This being my first car accident, combined with a sense of urgency to track down my vehicular assailant, I decided to try and drive around the block looking for the driver, all the while the metal on the side of my car digging into my tires causing smoke to rise. I was not able to track them down, however, and simply had to drive very slowly with my hazard lights on all the way back to the college campus.

Expect the Unexpected

My purpose in sharing this story is not to receive sympathy but rather to illustrate a particular truth. It serves as a perfect example of how something can happen in an instant to change the course of our day, month, year, even our entire life. I'm sure you can relate to my story. Maybe your circumstance was not a car accident. It could be the loss of a job or demotion within that job, being robbed or losing a loved one. The fact of the matter is, we all throughout life experience unexpected obstacles.

But, as different as each obstacle we face, our views and responses to such happenings are equally diverse. Some of us may take them as simply frustrating occurrences with neither rhyme nor reason; others may shake their fists at the sky and curse God, longing for a life with no problems, while still others may actually consider these "strange" moments agents that serve a greater purpose in our lives. The latter realize that most everything in life happens for a reason, and the purpose for the unforeseen obstacle may just be to develop some area of lack in their lives—as ludicrous as that may sound to natural human understanding.

A far better example of this principle than the story I told of my being blasted by a van, is the story of Job. Job was an upright and God-fearing man, and was also very wealthy. (Job 1:1) Job had it made: wealth, renown, wife, and children to carry on his legacy. Then, seemingly out of nowhere, something totally unexpected happened. His world was turned upside down in a matter of days.

The story goes that Satan came to God one day with a rant of accusation against Job, declaring that surely if God took everything away from him, he would no longer love, serve and worship God but would instead curse Him. And for whatever reason, God decided to accept Satan's challenge. First Job's servants and livestock were picked off. Then his children perished. Then, he was inflicted with physical ailment beyond comprehension—his body was covered with boils from head to toe. And finally, his own wife lost faith and told him he'd be better off to curse God and kill himself! (Job 1:1-2:10) In a matter of hours—a couple days total—everything he had was taken from him.

Yet, when we look at Job's response to this situation, we find something remarkable: an almost otherworldly perspective. He said, "Naked I came from my mother's womb, and naked I will depart. The LORD gave and the LORD has taken away; may the name of the LORD be praised." (1:21; NIV) And the Bible says further still, "In all this, Job did not sin by charging God with wrongdoing." (1:22; NIV)

Can you imagine experiencing the level of loss and affliction that Job did, and still giving praise to God? The depth of pain and depression he must have felt, and yet he seems thankful to still have breath in his lungs with which to praise God! I cannot tell you honestly without a doubt in my mind that I would have the same response given Job's circumstances. There is a good chance that praises wouldn't be the first words proceeding from my mouth but rather syllables I prefer not to even mention here in pen and ink.

Hope Deferred

There is another story from the Bible that beautifully illustrates a faith response in the most unexpected and unsettling circumstances. That is the story of King David, but before he became king. A good majority of David's life is often overlooked when his story is shared in sermons, books and movies. We all know he was called by God, killed a heathen giant with a sling-shot and became a mighty conquering king who made preparations for the grandiose House of God which his son Solomon was later appointed to construct.

But, there was a time in David's life—after kingship being promised to him, and before he actually became king—that is a crucial part of his story. God had both anointed David and called him to be king when he was a young man, a boy even (1 Samuel 16:13). And David even began to experience victories in his life that whispered kingly significance, as if he were steadily moving toward this calling of kingship. Yet, what seemed to be the beginning of an increasing closeness to the culmination of his calling was met with an unexpected and daunting obstacle.

After slaying the giant Goliath—when no one else was brave enough to face this blasphemous beast of a man—he entered into King Saul's service. Saul took kindly to David and brought him under his kingly wing so to speak. Now even more so it would seem David was on a course of steady progression toward Kingship. David even became best friends with Saul's son Jonathan.

Then it happened. Like a train wreck claiming unsuspecting lives, affliction and tribulation came full speed into David's life. Saul, under the influence of demonic forces began to detest David. But, it didn't stop with mere disapproval; Saul actually began attempts at taking David's life. Numerous times he tried to kill him, each time David narrowly escaping with his life. Things weren't going the way he'd hoped I'm sure. The promise and anointing once given him now were being threatened with dilution of doubt. The promise that once seemed to be so near on the horizon, now was fading into a distant hope that David must have begun to question whether it would ever come about.

For many years David ran and hid from Saul. It is remarkable that his response to not only God, but also Saul himself, in this situation was one of humility and surrender. It may seem obvious that he, being a man of great faith, would still have a heart after God in the midst of such trying times, but he even kept respect for Saul, the man who was trying to kill him! So much so that even when David—during the years of being pursued relentlessly by Saul—was presented with two perfect opportunities to take Saul's life, defending his calling and innocence, he refused and spared Saul's life. (1 Samuel 24, 26)

After many long, hard years that David was forced to endure, Saul was finally taken out of the picture. Justice was done and David finally became king. Even when Saul was dead however, David's response was still unselfish. He had every right to jump up and down singing songs of rejoicing over the elimination of this relentlessly oppressive enemy, who had kept him from pursuing his calling these many years. Quite to the contrary however, David did not rejoice, he mourned.

> "Then David and all the men with him took hold of their clothes and tore them. They **mourned and wept** and fasted till evening for Saul and his son Jonathan, and for the army of the LORD and for the nation of Israel, because they had fallen by the sword."
>
> 2 Samuel 1:11-12 (NIV)

David did not respond in a way that seems reasonable in any normal sense of the word. What we see is that his response is rather an echo of a faith-filled perspective not of this world. Because of his intimate connection with God, David was able to see his circumstance with eyes of faith and a heart filled with grace. He didn't hold a grudge against King Saul, or God, and the character that he developed as a result would be that of true kingly substance. Far more royal in its truest sense than ever could have been said of his malignant predecessor. We may think that Saul kept David from his calling, when in actuality, what David had to endure at the end of Saul's pursuant spear was a substance which helped further solidify David's calling and bring him to the fulfillment of promise.

Stuff Happens

Sometimes God allows us to be unpleasantly surprised by twists and turns in our lives. Now, these sudden occurrences may not be a work of the enemy, and then again, they may. That is not the point. It is not always necessary for us to try and determine whether it is merely random happenings or direct testing from the enemy (this does happen however, as was the case with Job). What matters most is our response. There is a reason we are going through the "test" and it may not be because we *have done something wrong*, but rather, that we *should do something right*.

The character, strength and wisdom that develops as result of properly dealing with these unexpected obstacles, could come to us no other way. Some lessons must be learned in the pits. If we refuse to faithfully see it through, the result could be stunting our own growth as well as missing out on innumerable blessings that could be freely ours. Like stubborn children who in refusing to eat their broccoli and cauliflower, forfeit that glorious dessert they so long for.

This Too Shall Pass

And there is dessert to be sure! Whether in this life or the next, we will experience bliss beyond comprehension if we endure through our struggles. Second Corinthians 4:17 says, "For our light and momentary troubles are achieving for us an eternal glory that far outweighs them all." (NIV) At first glance one might say, "My troubles aren't light! They're immense!" But to look closer at this verse, we see something different entirely than that. It is not minimizing our pain and suffering, but rather, our perspective is simply being balanced—if we allow this process to work in us. For when we compare our momentary troubles to the glory that awaits us for enduring through them, they do indeed appear much smaller than we thought them before. Not because they are small, so much as, the glory simply trumps them. Similar to the way the moon eclipses the sun.

Both Job and David had this kind of hope at work within them. There is no other way they could've endured what they did, unless they had something otherworldly working in them, something heavenly. And we see that their hope was not in vain. And they didn't even have to wait till after passing from this world to see some fulfillment of this hope. Job, after enduring a more difficult season of life than I could ever imagine, was abundantly rewarded for his faith. The Scriptures say:

> After Job had prayed for his friends, the LORD restored his fortunes and gave him twice as much as he had before. All his brothers and sisters and everyone who had known him before came and ate with him in his house. They comforted and consoled him over all the trouble the LORD had brought on him, and each one gave him a piece of silver and a gold ring. The LORD blessed the

> latter part of Job's life more than the former part. He had fourteen thousand sheep, six thousand camels, a thousand yoke of oxen and a thousand donkeys. And he also had seven sons and three daughters. The first daughter he named Jemimah, the second Keziah and the third Keren-Happuch. Nowhere in all the land were there found women as beautiful as Job's daughters, and their father granted them an inheritance along with their brothers. After this, Job lived a hundred and forty years; he saw his children and their children to the fourth generation. And so Job died, an old man and full of years.
>
> -Job 42:10-17 (NIV)

And David, well, he became king. God lavished upon him the favor and glory that he had longed for his entire life. He finally received the promise, which he had had to believe and fight for through the most disheartening of circumstances. He did not fall back from the promise, but he held on to hope in the face of adversity. His faith proved true, and was in turn rewarded. Oh, and I almost forgot to tell you how my story turned out. Though for a time my wallet, body and vehicle suffered as a result of the accident, it actually turned out to be a blessing in disguise.

I was provided with two weeks of free chiropractic therapy from my insurance company, as well as a settlement of almost $2,000! Being a broke college student, that much goes a long way! Before the accident, I had a large dent with rust developing near the gas tank of my car, which is right where I was hit. So, when I received my car back—post $4,500 in repairs, of which I only paid a $500 deductable—it was actually in much better shape than before! And to top the dessert with a nice red cherry, I was able to drive a "fire-red" 2007 Ford Mustang for two weeks at a cost of next to nothing. My insurance covered 80% of it.

You may wonder why I shared all this. You might be thinking, oh, how all this even compares with the stories of Job and David. But this is why: I believe God is involved in every detail of our lives. He bears a personal interest in each and every moment, not just the big stuff, but little things too. And besides, seemingly small trials—getting in a car accident for instance—are not small at all when we are in them. It was a big deal to me, thus, I believe it was a big deal to God. He was allowing me to go through a tough time so that I could learn and grow, and so that I could share the story with you now of His faithfulness.

The Big Question

Some may ask "why". Why did God allow Job, and David—along with countless others throughout history—to go through such loss and pain? To which we may only receive one response: "What is that to you? You must follow me." (John 21:22; NIV) And though this may sound like somewhat of a cop-out, it is sometimes the only response we receive. Simply another reminder that the question we should really be asking is not, "Why?" But rather, "What?" As in, "What do you want me to do, Lord?" This is the way Job and David ultimately responded. Yes, we see plenty of asking "why" in their words—just look at the Psalms David wrote—nevertheless, if we take a full-scope view of their life, we see they didn't stay in the "why". They moved on in faith to the "what". Restoration and glory was the result.

So here we are now, faced with a choice: will we keep shaking our fist at the sky begging the question, "Why?" Or will we bring ourselves face to face with our difficult and alarming circumstances, declaring that we will do whatever is asked of us in order to make it through to a greater faith? The choice is ours to make. Either decision is equally available to us. Though one calls our name a little quieter than the other.

Faith speaks softly to our hearts but reaps a lasting and eternal strength, which far outweighs our doubts, fears and hesitations when we let it. Whilst all the time doubts, fears and questionings of God's goodness shout in our face, declaring that pouting, complaining and frustration are in fact the most reasonable responses to our circumstances. But, we must look deeper than our impulses in order to respond in faith. We must draw upon the inner strength that the Spirit of God lavishes within us so freely. He is our only hope for getting through it rightly.

This is what we learn from the stories of Job and David, that the only way out of the surprising obstacles, which are inevitable in life, is directly through them. We must proceed *through* the fiery trials, as there is no way around them. And we also learn that it is only the solidity of our relationship with God that will get us through. This is how they did it. They always came back around to their one true love, the only One who could help them in their great sorrow and distress.

God is the only one who both knows all and has power over all. Though we may have no clue whatsoever why we must endure our present circumstances, He does; He can see the whole picture, we only see a snippet. Just like the analogy of the person peeking through a small whole in a fence to see the parade go by. We can only see a piece at a time. But, like the helicopter floating high above the parade, God can see the whole thing—our whole life, not just this momentary affliction—from start to finish. And He alone has the power to intervene.

"Then why doesn't He do something sooner?" we may ask. But there we go again, asking the wrong question. God is not obliged to tell us why He does what He does. All that we are required to know is, that He is good and cares for all people with equal love and affection—though it may appear sometimes as otherwise. To illustrate, simply look at any of the good parents that you can think of. Truly good parents love their children unconditionally, but sometimes they allow their children to experience things of their own accord. The parents know that either by not being able to watch the children every moment of every day, or simply by intention of teaching a lesson, they are expressing their love for the child and training them up rightly.

Take for example when a child bonks his head on the corner of the kitchen table, or when a bee that he was attempting to capture in a mason jar stings him. Sometimes we must experience hardship, hurt and sorrow in order to be toughened up, if you will. And not only this, but we also learn about things that require more caution, or even avoidance. The pot boiling atop the stove for instance: once we touch it for the first time and singe our fragile little fingers, it is highly unlikely that we will repeat the same mistake.

For someone to say, or even imply, that God is not a good God simply because He allows bad things to happen, is both a misunderstanding and blatantly ignorant conclusion. It would not be love for the parent to always protect the child from every kind of harm, let alone that this would be even be possible for an earthly parent. Love lets you experience life for yourself. Still standing by at the ready to protect you, but not from every little painful experience.

God allows us to experience these peculiar twists and unexpected obstacles so that we can learn, and so that our faith will grow stronger in the process. He wants us to both take Him at His word *and* experience it firsthand. He will never leave us alone, but He will not bail us out of every difficult situation we face either. Some He will, others He won't. And this is not a decision that is up to us to make. Again, He sees the whole parade; we see only a tiny piece at a time—the piece that is happening right now. Who then do we think is better suited for the major decisions in our lives about what we need and don't need to experience.

When faced with surprising obstacles that seem impossible to get through, and all I want to do is wallow in sorrow and surrender to a victim mentality, I must look instead upon the hope held out in the word of God. I must remember that these "light" and momentary trials are working in me something that will last, and driving me toward a greater glory than could ever be imagined.

- Chapter 9 -

The Great Beyond: Glorious Shore

"There will come a day, you'll see, with no more tears.

And love will not break your heart, but dismiss your fears."

-Mumford & Sons, *After the Storm*

- Chapter 9 -

The Great Beyond: Glorious Shore

I remember visiting my grandfather one last time before his passing in the spring of 2007. As my family and I walked the long halls of the hospice where he was being kept, slowly approaching his room, I was oblivious to the fact that a radical spiritual experience was about to be thrust upon me. Being the zealous and fresh young Christian man that I was, I rather expected that I would be the one to minister to him. How wrong I was. What came next took all speech from me; anything that I had previously prepared to say flew right out the window of my mind leaving only a silent moment of awe to be basked in.

Upon reaching my grandfather's room—really, room isn't quite the right word, as it was more of a hospital chamber—we came upon him lying in a very "sanitary" hospital bed with a sort of distant, although grateful, look on his face as he greeted us. He was obviously very happy to see us, but it was plain to see he was somewhat detached from reality. Well, reality as in this earthly realm, however, that in no way means crazy. Actually, he was much closer in this moment to a greater reality, one I believe to be more real than this world.

I had recently bought a new—though old fashioned—fine driving cap that I was wearing at the moment, and I thought it might bring him some sort of comfort for him to hold it and give me his approval of this fine cap. And he did enjoy looking it over and running his fingers over the plaid patterned wool; it appeared to be somewhat therapeutic as we tried to hold a conversation with him.

I remember a couple times during our feeble attempts to hold his attention, he would suddenly look toward the ceiling and begin breaking down in a sort of blissful joy. He began proclaiming, in a very childlike simplicity and affection, "Oh! Jesus, my Jesus! My sweet, sweet Jesus! So beautiful!" And, "Oh, the music! OH! The music!" He would say as tears of joy began rolling off his cheeks, and his eyes were lit up like a little boy at Christmas.

During this magnificent display of otherworldly affection that my grandfather was expressing—almost involuntarily—toward God, I was taken aback. You must understand, I had never seen my grandfather so passionate and excited about simple intimacy with Jesus. Sure, he talked about God a lot and was even a Reverend of a Lutheran Church for many years, but I had never seen anything like this. The nurses that attended my grandfather, being that they had only just met him in this state, if they were given the task of guessing his Christian denomination might have thought him to be a Charismatic Pentecostal! And this I mean in the most respectful sense.

Now, don't hear what I'm not saying: I am not going to begin discussing the benefits and detriments of any given denomination, nor pick on the differences, good or bad, between them. That is not my point in sharing this story. And it is not the goal of this book to push you, the reader, in any particular direction regarding denomination. Rather, my main purpose in sharing this wonderful moment with you is to bring a greater attention to something that far outweighs anything of this world. I want to bring to the forefront what my grandfather experienced in that moment: a simple childlike awe and wonder so overwhelming that it couldn't be contained. Every distinguished reserve that my grandfather might have held before was tossed to the breeze as all that mattered in that moment was running to Jesus and being overtaken by the unspeakably glorious music of heaven.

My grandfather was actually seeing glimpses of heaven, and more specifically, Jesus calling him home. It only makes sense then that a matter of days later, he did in fact pass on, and I believe, went home to be with the Lord. To be that near with someone so close, so connected with heaven, is something truly life-changing. I will never forget the overwhelming expression of joy and heavenly anticipation on my grandfather's face as he began transitioning from this world to the next. In that moment, it was like there was a tangible connection between heaven and earth, and with it an undeniable feeling of inexplicable glory.

Beyond Words

As I watched my grandfather that day, lying there on his hospital bed, looking to the sky in wonder, something became very clear to me. When one comes face to face with the King of kings and the glorious sound of heaven, nothing else matters. All else that is of such great concern in life becomes a mere blur in comparison with the glory that awaits in that heavenly Home.

One day, as the Bible says, Jesus will return to take His own unto Him. And, in that moment, I believe we will be much like my grandfather at his passing: completely overwhelmed by the glory of God in an uncontrolled compulsion of affection for Him. We will not, in that moment, try and reason with God inquiring with Him how well we did with our life on earth. We will not be the ones to initiate that, God will. In that moment, we will see God, unveiled, as pure glory—glory that is impossible to describe with mere human words. It is not something that can be described accurately in man's terminology. Rather, we will be thrust headfirst into it as an experiential culmination far beyond all knowledge we accumulated while living on earth.

This is not some idea fabricated from human imagination; we see it clearly illustrated in the Word of God. Whenever someone would try to write about visions they had received of heaven, they would try to grab all the earthly words they could to illustrate what they had seen. What we perceive from this is that it was ultimately impossible. Why do you think the Book of Revelation is so difficult to understand? Why Ezekiel and Daniel's writings seem so cryptic? When God reveals something of heaven to man, man then attempts to retell the tale and it sounds either like nonsense or something way too complicated to grasp—or both at the same time. And though with extensive research and study the mysteries of these sections of Scripture can become clearer, there will always be elements that are completely out of our reach to our present ability of understanding; things of another world, which can only be understood within the context of that world. The purpose for them then is not for us to understand, so much as to keep us in our place. The mysteries declare to us the incomprehensible glory of God.

Though most of what heaven will be like is out of reach to our comprehension now, that does not mean we don't have some specific things to look forward to. I believe there are things we will experience which can be understood enough at present to bring great encouragement and anticipation for our true Home as followers of Christ.

Paradigm Shift

I have never liked little baby Cherubs. Every time I see sculptures and paintings of little naked babies with wings, my eye begins to twitch a little. Now, from a purely artistic perspective, sure I can appreciate the expression. But, the reason these little winged children bother me so much is because they insinuate some illusory idea that is simply not Biblically sound. For one thing, whenever an Angel is mentioned in Scripture, the appearance of such a being is the furthest thing from cute and cuddly. Rather, those who beheld such entities were cast to the ground in awe and holy fear. The way they are described are as glorious and mighty warriors, much more resembling a glorified man than a little babe.

Another way that these illustrations misconstrue the truths of heavenly things is that they give the idea of heaven being all sitting on clouds playing our little harps—again, a very cute and cuddly view of heaven. To me this is insulting. These artistic misconceptions are not Biblical and hold no ground for what heaven and Angels are actually like, thank God! Now, if you are one who likes these little Cherubs and artistic expressions of reclining on cloud-fluff for all eternity, please do not take it that I am telling you to toss all of this baby Cherub paraphernalia in the trash bin. My purpose is solely to combat wrong thinking and get us to view these dynamic elements of the Afterlife rightly—as Scripture, not art, puts forth.

Early in my faith I remember struggling with this issue. I didn't give a whole lot of thought to what heaven would actually be like, and thus whenever it was brought to my attention—either in conversation or moments of reflection—I was at a loss for words. And by no means have I come to a full understanding these many years later. As I said a bit earlier, the issue of the Great Beyond is something we will never understand, until we are actually in it. Thus, it is safe to believe we all struggle to grasp what it will be like. At least we know it will not be boring, contrary to what the little baby Cherubs on fluffy clouds would have us believe.

Now, if we are going to endeavor to understand what can be understood—at least to an extent—about it, we must get past all of our preconceived notions. Things like I illustrated previous, things like little baby Angels on fluffy clouds and sitting around playing harps all day, every day for the rest of eternity. And it doesn't stop there. The little Cherubs I would say are the least of our worries in comparison to some other ideas people hold about heaven and how to get there. Some of these world views—or should I say "after-world views"—are downright disturbing when held to the light of Scripture. And it is very interesting that many of these other religions actually bear some hints of Christianity, as if they all borrowed from it. But, even if a belief system has a little bit of truth in it, the man-made philosophies serve as weak links which cause the whole thing to crumble—like a house made of sand.

Mormons—AKA Latter Day Saints—believe you will go to not one of two places (heaven or hell) but rather, one of SIX places! And that in the highest of these places called "The Church of the Firstborn" a person will actually achieve Godhood—become a god.[25] In some Eastern religions and New Age belief systems, Reincarnation is held as the crux of the faith—acceptable I suppose if your hope of glory is being birthed as a squirrel or centipede in your next life.[26] Jehovah Witnesses claim to believe in the Bible as authoritative yet deny the existence of hell, but that the condemned will be annihilated, which sounds like a much more favorable sentence than what the Bible actually teaches us about hell. They do believe in a sort of heaven but that only 144,000 will get to see it and rule with Christ—as you well know I'm sure, is a number that has been passed some time ago—and the rest will simply experience a new Eden on earth.[27] And there is a broad sea of other beliefs out there on what heaven, or lack thereof, will be like. But I will spare you; this is after all, ultimately a book about Christianity, which is where I choose to spend the most time and effort. It is more important, I believe, to focus on the right view, than on all the wrong ones.

The reason I shared all of this is to simply show how easily we humans can get wrong ideas and odd philosophies about the afterlife. So, in order to proceed to a greater understanding, we must push back everything that would get in the way. We must clear our minds and hold tightly only to what the Bible teaches about heaven and hell. It is not up to us to decide what we do and do not like about this issue. What is done is done, what is written is written and will never change. It is my belief that this is where all these strange ideas about heaven come from, people who stray from the Word of God and set up there own belief system. Like rebellious children, who pick and choose what they do and don't like about something and then set that up as their ideal, their truth. But, that is not how it works. You cannot change truth, it is what it is through and through; there is no possibility of alteration to it. No matter how much we think we can believe whatever we want about heaven and hell, the truth remains, and it is unchanged. It is what it is, and that is what it will be. We only have two choices: to believe that it is what the Word says about it, or to disbelieve and one day discover we were wrong—to our own great sorrow.

Randy Alcorn, in his book entitled *Heaven* challenges all people to think more about heaven, and not just that, but more *accurately* about it. He says, "It's our inaccurate thinking, I believe, that causes us to choose to think so little about heaven."[28] This is a profound statement. How often do we think of heaven? And when we do, what is it we think about? How do we view the afterlife? What is our expectancy? I know for me, when there is something I am greatly looking forward to, something that holds immensely great benefit for me: that is a thing that will permeate my thoughts. Likened to a romantic relationship in first bloom, the thought of uniting your heart, soul and body with another is a hope that will completely consume you. Day and night, you cannot stop thinking about that person, and you can't wait to spend time with them again. You are willing to go to great lengths just to spend a few fleeting moments together.

What if our view of heaven became like that? What if instead of viewing heaven as this boring place where we sit on clouds with harps—or whatever other corrupted idea of it may come—we actually saw it the way God wants us to, the way He intended? Suddenly we are faced with a new frontier of understanding, a fresh hope for the afterlife. It will be a great adventure beyond all imagination: unspeakable wonders, bliss, fulfillment, life, as it has never been felt before. This is the kind of heaven I am looking forward to, and it is something that constantly consumes my thoughts—not with dread, but rather with the greatest joy and anticipation. At times it is necessary for me to challenge my own perspective, as I often grow a little too fond of this world, but after a moment or two of reflection, I realize once again how my earthly abode pales in comparison to that heavenly dwelling that is being prepared for me.

Fulfillment

"Until the sea of glass we meet
At last completed and complete
Where tide and tear and pain subside
And laughter drinks them dry."

-Switchfoot, *Restless*

Do you feel an unfulfilled longing for accomplishing many different things in this life? Do you have certain dissatisfaction with what you are doing now? Maybe you want to do so much more but are hindered by the thought of doing everything you'd like to do. If you're like me, you can probably relate. I am the type of person that has so many aspirations and not near enough time or energy to fulfill all of my desires, no matter how noble they may be.

This makes me wonder; maybe the reason so many things we'd like to do in this life are left undone is simply because we aren't meant to do them all. Could it be that our passion to accomplish so many things, even for the Kingdom of God, is simply a "hint of heaven"? That we should simply do each assignment God gives us with a sort of holy dissatisfaction—a longing for that Home which is yet to come. Appreciating every moment and even being thankful for the un-fulfillment of many desires in order that we might gain a right perspective of life on earth—that it is temporary. We need to remember that we have an eternal home in which all righteous longings and yet so much more than we can imagine shall be fulfilled. It will be an eternal, never-ending fulfillment, continuous in a land with no time, money, relational, inspirational, emotional, physical or spiritual restraint. We will be in the glory of God forever. No more longing, only fulfillment.

Does this not sound like something almost too wonderful to imagine? And that is just what we have to look forward to: a heavenly Home where all of our greatest longings are ultimately fulfilled. No more waiting, no more trying to squeeze every productive activity we can into such a short span of time. For time itself will cease to exist. We will no longer view our lives in hours, months and years. It will be like one continuous glorious moment of pure joy and holy satisfaction that will never end.

Work (as a gift)

Work is usually something that we dread returning to every Monday. No matter how many benefits you receive, your job is still a job that, given the choice, you would probably rather do something else. And why is that? Well, it only makes sense if we look back to the beginning, when sin entered the world, when Paradise was spoiled and lost. God said, "Cursed is the ground because of you; *through painful toil* you will eat food from it all the days of your life. It will produce *thorns and thistles* for you, and you will eat the plants of the field. By the *sweat of your brow* you will eat your food until you return to the ground, since from it you were taken; for dust you are and to dust you will return." (Genesis 3:17-19; NIV)

The reason we don't fully enjoy work on earth is because of this "curse" from God, which was initiated by man's fall from righteousness. Ever since then, man has had to work, and by work, I mean, work HARD. This is why we don't enjoy showing up to our jobs every day and staying until our shift is over. This is why there is an underlying dissatisfaction with the work we do: it takes "painful toil," "sweat" and enduring "thorns and thistles". None of these things are enjoyable. But I think you would agree there is still some tiny remnant of joy within our work. There are shining moments when we thoroughly enjoy our job—though often brief. Moments when we realize we are helping someone, or doing something worthwhile. Like a small flame flickering in a large darkened room, we sense a bit of warmth and light that encourages us to press on. A tiny feeling inside that we are experiencing a little, if only a fleck, of that which we were made for.

This is a hint of heaven, a little piece of that which we will experience in its entirety when once we are Home. It is a gift from God, or rather, a promise—or seal—of what is to come. It is these little hints, which when taken hold of and dwelt upon, can drive us forward with a new perspective. We then realize that our occupation in heaven will be like a quilt that is crafted by all these bits and pieces—brief moments of joy in our earthly work. No longer will the moments be few and spread apart, they will be close-knit with no space in-between and as widespread as all eternity. There will be work in heaven, but nothing like we have ever known. We will not be working for a paycheck, but rather simply because it is what we are made for. The fulfillment and overwhelming sense of purpose will be inexplicably wonderful

New Bodies

"But our citizenship is in heaven, and from it we await a Savior, the Lord Jesus Christ, who will *transform our lowly body to be like his glorious body*, by the power that enables him even to subject all things to himself." (Philippians 3:20-21; NIV) And again the Word says, "So will it be with the resurrection of the dead. The body that is sown is perishable, it is raised imperishable; it is sown in dishonor, it is raised in glory; it is sown in weakness, it is raised in power; it is sown a natural body, it is raised a spiritual body." (1 Corinthians 15:42-44; NIV) Think of it; we will have new bodies! This is almost too wonderful to comprehend. No longer will these frail earthen vessels bind us. We will be transformed completely.

In chapter two, "The Unseen You", I shared about "that-which-lasts"—that the real us is not this physical body, or casing, but rather what is underneath, the unseen us. And in chapter four, "Neo-Genesis", I illustrated the importance of transformation, which occurs at the time of giving one's life to Jesus—upon receiving salvation. This however, is a whole other level entirely. I am not just speaking about the internal change that occurs with your "inner-self"—the change that affects your mind, will and emotions; the change which transfers you from the kingdom of darkness to the Kingdom of Light. What we are now brought to look upon is something far more incredible. It is the complete culmination and completion of our salvation.

At that time, the transformation will run its full course. There will be no more sin nature in us, it will be completely removed. We will be *like* Christ: perfect. Sickness, depression, loneliness, sorrow, pain, and conflict: all imperfections and ailments will be done away with. Running out of energy, being bed ridden, injuries, and migraines will be no more. We won't have to worry about forgetting important appointments, and whether we bought enough groceries. Our bodies will no longer depend upon food; rather, eating will be only for the purpose of pure enjoyment. I can only imagine what food will taste like in heaven: no contaminants, toxins, or preservatives. And our sense of taste and smell will be out of this world, literally.

As you can see, the subject of our future transfigured heavenly state is one I am quite fond of. Often, when I am struggling to muster up enough strength just to make it through another day, or when I am battling sickness or pain in my body, or when depression and loneliness strike a shattering blow, I simply reflect on how one day I will no longer be confined to this frail body but will have a new and perfect one. God makes available to us His power and grace and strengthens us while we are still here on earth—bound by our mortal bodies—but how much greater an experience shall it be when once we are fully transformed, shedding forever these skins that have kept us so limited, never to put them back on again.

Friendship

"That it ever should have been doubted whether the inhabitants of the spiritual world recognize each other in that abode is but an example of the wide influence of unbelief, suggesting the strangest dimness wherever the Scriptures had not spoken in the most explicit words, even though the obvious reason for which the words had not been spoken was, that to speak them was needless."
-RT. REV. GEO. Burgess D. D.[29]

Another incredible element of heaven that we can look forward to is friendship. How wonderful a thing it is here on earth, and how much more so in our true Homeland! Think of all the good in friendships and none of the bad. That is what it will be like.

Though we will be transformed—transfigured may be an even better, fuller word—we will not be unrecognizable to those whom we knew on earth. Nor will we be unknown to those who we never met, who will be there as well. All the Patriarchs, Prophets and Kings who ascended to heaven wait for us there with a foreknowledge of who we are. For we are all one body of believers, both those departed and those still dwelling on earth.

This is very encouraging. After all, I'm sure to not be the only one who ever wondered whether I would see and know my family, my friends, and my spouse in heaven. Why would we not? Though we may take on a glorified body, our distinguishing uniqueness will not be done away with. When Adam and Eve were created perfect, they had distinguishable faces, which I don't believe changed when sin entered the world—except for the natural process of aging, which had then begun to run its course. Why then would it be any different the other way round? Why would our faces change when once sin departs forever from us? Rather, I believe we will look *more* like ourselves than we ever have before—the real us, the appearance of our true image which is only dimly reflected upon the face of our earthly vessel at present. As we were created: in the image of God, more specifically, Christ.

But not only will we be known by those we love—and *all* people in heaven, even those we don't yet know—we will have a fellowship with them in the Presence of God like nothing we've ever known. Relationship between people has been something so dear to the heart of God from the beginning of time, that He placed it on an almost equal plane with the first and greatest Commandment. The only thing that is above it is our relationship with God Himself.

> "Hearing that Jesus had silenced the Sadducees, the Pharisees got together. One of them, an expert in the law, tested him with this question: "Teacher, which is the greatest commandment in the Law?" Jesus replied: "'Love the Lord your God with all your heart and with all your soul and with all your mind.'- This is the first and greatest commandment. *And the second is like it: 'Love your neighbor as yourself.'* All the Law and the Prophets hang on these two commandments."
>
> -Matthew 22:34-40 (NIV; *italics mine*)

How then could an unchanging God demand anything different when once we reach heaven than what He demands from us while we're on earth—unless it is something even loftier, holier? Thus we can conclude that friendship in heaven will be even greater, infinitely greater, than it is here on earth. There will be no more quarrelling or arguments, no disappointments or hang-ups, no insults, yelling, or slamming doors; no gossip, no misconceptions, misinterpretations and misunderstandings; there will be only pure, concentrated, one hundred percent love-filled friendship. Something we cannot grasp here on earth no matter how hard we try, but can still hope for with great expectancy when once we are Home.

Worship

This is an area that I used to have an issue with; as a matter of fact, I still do sometimes. My perspective regarding the activity of heavenly worship must constantly be challenged and brought back to the truth of God's Word, and not my own understanding of what it might be like. What do you think of when the Bible talks about worshiping God night and day in heaven without ceasing? I believe, like every other aspect of the message of heaven, we must view it accurately in order to get excited about it.

The problem I always had when I heard that we would worship God day and night was that it sounded like a never-ending Church service. Now, don't get me wrong, I love being in Church, but not all day every day! There are so many other things I enjoy doing, so many adventures to be had outside of the four walls. And I think these are things God desires for us to enjoy. What is worship anyway? We learn from the Bible that it isn't just singing along with the song lyrics on the screen Sunday morning or Wednesday evening—it's so much more than that. The Bible puts it this way…

> "And so, dear brothers and sisters, I plead with you to give your bodies to God because of all he has done for you. Let them be a living and holy sacrifice—the kind he will find acceptable. *This is truly the way to worship him.*"
>
> -Romans 12:1 (NLT)

So we see from this Scripture, worship is not only singing songs to God with our vocal chords, but rather, with our very lives. In all we do and say, in the way we offer our every day life to Him, this is the truest form of worship. Thus, in every activity, every moment of fellowship, every stroll down the Streets of Gold, we will be worshiping God in everything we do. But it doesn't stop there.

There is something that I will call "heightened moments of worship". What I mean is simply this: there are moments when we may be singing a song to God—of thankfulness, surrender, adoration or whatever reason there may be—and suddenly there is a tingle, and an almost trance-like feeling; there is a sense of connectedness and closeness to God that supersedes the norm. This can happen almost anywhere: your car, walking down the street, but especially in a church service that welcomes the Presence of God with open arms.

Now, this feeling, or sensation that comes in the midst of moments like this is completely overwhelming in the best meaning of the word. In a moment of "heightened" worship, when the Presence of God is truly *felt*, nothing else matters. You could have had the worst day of your life, or been completely uninterested in God before this occurrence. You may have, earlier on in the service, or during the course of your day, been incredibly distracted from God by all the responsibilities and demands of life, but in this moment, you couldn't care less about anything but God.

So, in regard to worship in heaven, this is what I think it will be like. A constant state of the felt (manifest) Presence of God, so breathtaking and wonderful, that nothing else will matter. We will never want to leave! And getting distracted by other things wouldn't even be an issue, because in our glorified bodies will we not have perfect focus—something we can only long for at present? Thus, even if heaven were a never-ending worship service, it wouldn't matter, because everything that causes us to dislike that idea would no longer be in existence. With drowsiness, distractions, worries of life and so on out of the picture, an eternal moment of singing songs to God would be pure bliss. But this again takes thinking in otherworldly terms. It is not something easily processed in our current earthly state. For, it is true, even as I am speaking on these things, you are possibly being distracted, becoming drowsy or simply disinterested in the idea altogether. Only further proving it is not something we can fully comprehend at present.

We Will See Him Face to Face

"Now we see but a poor reflection as in a mirror; then we shall see face to face. Now I know in part; then I shall know fully,
even as I am fully known."
-1 Corinthians 13:12 (NIV)

I have saved the best for last. Of all that we have to look forward to, out of everything we've discussed and the countless other wonders we haven't, this one thing is by far the most important, and the crux upon which all that is hoped for is placed. Beyond all comprehension, by far the greatest wonder of heaven is that we will see Jesus face-to-face, in person, up close and personal, in the fullness of His glory. This is nigh unspeakable, and no amount of words—earthly or heavenly—could fully describe the beauty that moment will hold.

Throughout our days of faith on earth, we pray continually to an invisible God, a person we cannot see. The only ones who have actually seen Jesus were the people who lived in the Middle East two thousand years ago, though even they did not see Him in all His glory; no one who is human has ever seen Him thus. But on that Great Day, we will. It will be a face-to-face encounter with our Savior and Creator, our Redeemer and our God. For those who know the Lord and await His return with joy, this moment will be the most wonderful experience in the history of the universe. It will be the completion of the greatest love story ever told, a completion that never ends. It is a Happily Ever After like which has never been known. And at that time we, I believe, much like my grandfather, will be completely overwhelmed in childlike simplicity, by the all encompassing beauty of seeing our Savior in the flesh.

"When we arrive at Eternity's shore
Where death is just a memory and tears are no more
We'll enter in as wedding bells ring
Your Bride will come together and we'll sing
You're Beautiful, You're Beautiful, You're Beautiful."
-Phil Wickam, *Beautiful*

- Chapter 10 -

The Great Beyond II: Terrible Abyss

"In Hades, where he was in torment, he looked up and saw
Abraham far away, with Lazarus by his side. So he called to him,
'Father Abraham, have pity on me and send Lazarus to dip the tip
of his finger in water and cool my tongue,
because I am in agony in this fire."

-Luke 16:23-24 (NIV)

- Chapter 10 -

The Great Beyond II: Terrible Abyss

Hell. We don't really like that word very much, at least, in its literal sense. This is really no surprise when one realizes the truth about such a place. You see it was never intended for man to go there. God did not create hell so that He could punish humans; He created it as a punishment to fallen angels, namely, Lucifer. And this I believe is why, when we hear the word hell, we usually feel a little uneasy. It is not a place we were created for, it is not natural for us. Nevertheless, regardless of the uncomfortable nature of discussions on hell, it would be to the neglect of our spiritual well being to never discuss it at all. We must know what this place really is like, and why God intends that no one should have to go there. This will help us also have a much greater appreciation for the wonder that awaits us in heaven, for when the two are accurately contrasted side-by-side, there is no comparison or issue of choosing. We will only want to choose heaven.

A Few Misconceptions

Much like the topic of heaven, there are also numerous wrong ideas about hell. One of the many bad ideas about hell is that if we are people who enjoy being bad, we will have friends in hell. For instance, the man who says, "Well, at least I'll be in good company." But, this is a severe misconception. As John Bevere pointed out in his book *Driven By Eternity*, camaraderie will not exist in hell for it is a good thing, and no good thing will be in hell. Good will only be in heaven.[30] Though a simple truth, it is often brushed over and misconstrued and one of the primary issues I would like to get out of the way right off the bat.

Think of it: will there be friendly discussions with the Devil over a drink at the local Inferno Pub on the streets of Hades? Hardly. The devil, as we have discussed in previous chapters, is evil personified. He is corruption to the core. There is no goodness in him whatsoever. Any goodness he had once upon a time has now been thoroughly spoiled, and all that remains is the filth of wickedness. Thus, if we could not even imagine having a civilized conversation over drinks with the devil, how could we ever come to the ridiculous conclusion that we would have the commodity of "friends" in that place?

Another strange idea about hell is that it is run by the devil, that he is the king of sorts in that domain. Though this may bear some truth for the current state of the condemned, at present we are ultimately discussing the time after Jesus' return, AKA the end of the world. At that time, the Bible tells us all fallen angels, and humans who never entered a relationship with Christ, will be cast into the "lake of fire". Without going into extreme theological detail and discussion on this subject, we can gain some great insights on what it will actually be like.

The Bible describes the lake of fire as eternal torment (Revelation 20:10; 20:15; 21:8), not only for humans, but for devils as well, and that includes Satan himself. We must ask ourselves a question: if Satan himself, the epitome of evil—and a very powerful being at that (remember, he still has the power God bestowed upon him when he was an angel of heaven, as we discussed in The Anonymous Killer)—would be in utter torment in this place, how bad do you think it will be for humans? Hopefully that statement helps to put a little proper perspective on the subject.

You see, this coming judgment—hell if you want to call it that; more theologically specific: the lake of fire—is eternal punishment for all who have fallen, both demons and humans alike. No one is exempt who has been sent there. There are no ranks in the lake of fire; human and supernatural entity alike will be equally tormented for all eternity. Sounds pretty horrible right? And as it should. Again, this is not a place God intends for people to go.

> The Lord is not slow in keeping his promise, as some understand slowness. Instead he is patient with you, **not wanting anyone to perish**, but everyone to come to repentance.
>
> -2 Peter 3:9 (NIV; *emphasis mine*)

I once had a revelation about this. It is almost as if God does not actually send anyone to hell, but when the way they live their lives attaches them to evil, they cannot help but be damned right along with the angels that fell. Sin has a way of attaching itself to us and literally dragging us down, and unless we cry out for a Savior—unless we repent—there is no hope of being released from the grasp of evil, and the end result, as Scripture clearly says, is death. (Romans 6:23) There is no other way around it.

A Few Comparisons

In the last chapter, we discussed many elements of heaven that are things to look forward to, things that no matter what your religious background is, or what your worldview, they strike a positive chord somewhere in your heart. It is my belief that hell is the polar opposite of heaven, and as such, anything that was discussed in the last chapter—as well as any other positive elements that I failed to mention—would be completely on the other side of the spectrum.

If in heaven we find the greatest sense of fulfillment and purpose, then in hell—namely the lake of fire—there will be a holistic un-fulfillment. It will be like an eternal void: a lacking and longing that can never be filled. The only chance we have for filling the void in our hearts is while we still occupy this world. Only if we repent now and our names are written in the Book of Life can we have any hope of fulfillment. Once Jesus returns, or if we die before that Day, there will be no second chances; the choice will have already been made.

Can you imagine? Even now, while we live out our days on earth, the feeling of not being fulfilled, of having no purpose in life is almost too great to bear. I once was having a conversation with a good Japanese friend of mine while still in Bible College, and I asked him, "What would you say is the primary issue in Japanese culture today? What is it that the Japanese, especially youth, need to hear?" You know what he said? He said, "They need to know they have a purpose." We went on to discuss how that could be directly related to the high volume of suicides that occur in Japan. That would possibly explain why so many young people are taking their own lives: because they are overwhelmed by a sense that their lives are worth nothing.

Now, multiply that feeling of purposelessness and emptiness by a million, trillion, infinity. In hell, and in the lake of fire, there will be a level of emptiness that has never been felt before. And this crippling and excruciating feeling will go on forever, it will never end. Those who commit suicide in this life because of this feeling—or a very small dose of it—think that taking their own life is the only escape, that they will soon find relief from their sorrows. This is a deception. But we won't address that issue right now. Instead, I would like to focus on the simple fact that there will be no possibility of committing suicide in hell to try and escape from the emotional torture, it will be eternally absolute. Once it starts, it will never end.

Let us make some further comparisons. If work in heaven will be the substance of joy, then the work—or lack thereof—in hell, will be the material of sheer turmoil. If heaven will have all the bad taken out of work, hell will have all the good taken out. Any inkling of enjoyment you have ever felt while working in this world, though imperfect, would be something a man would be willing to trade anything for in hell. However, it is futile. Again, at that time, there will be no alternatives for those who are condemned.

And what about our bodies? If those who ascend to heaven receive new and glorious bodies, what will the bodies of those damned to Hades be like? If all pain, weariness, injury, illness and such will be done away with beyond the "pearly gates", what will those who are tossed into the terrible below be subjected to? I think it is safe to assume that it will again be completely opposite to the glory of heaven. Pain: terrible, unimaginable and excruciating pain will be all that is felt. In the "second death" as the Bible calls it (Revelation 21:8; NIV), there will be no relief from pain. It is a death that will continue forever.

The Bible actually talks of it this way: as a fire that never stops consuming. Can you imagine? How bad does it feel when you get one little burn on your finger? It pesters you for days! How much more the blazing fires of hell that will never go out? The Bible also mentions a "worm that never dies". John Bevere again in his book *Driven By Eternity* brings up an interesting, though disturbing point. Being that worms would literally devour your insides and flesh, if the worm never dies, that means it would continually need something to feed on. This would simply mean that a person's flesh would continue growing back so that the worm could keep feeding again and again.[31] Like I said, disturbing. But he presents a powerful point on how terrible it will be.

> "...where their worm does not die, and the fire is not quenched."
>
> -Mark 9:46 (NASB)

We have already briefly touched on the subject of friendship in hell: that it will be non-existent. How tragic it will be for those who will never again see their loved ones. They will have a constant longing to once again look upon their family members and friends, but to no avail. And don't for a second buy into the belief that the occupants of hell will not remember. The forgetting of sorrowful memories is a luxury of heaven, something foreign to the netherworld.

What of worship, the music of heaven? If the sound of heaven is more glorious and wonderful than anything ever happening upon human ears—or any ears for that matter—then the sound of hell will be quite the opposite. Think of all the most horrible sounds you can imagine, combined into one awful chorus and played like a broken record forevermore. An onslaught to the eardrums of blood curdling screams, the sound of torment, of torture. The joy that music brought while on the earth—again, though imperfect—will be long gone, never again reachable. Let alone the music of heaven. There will be no hope of EVER hearing that.

And now we come to the worst of all. Those who are sentenced to an eternal death in hell will be forever separated from God. Never again will any good—as all good comes from God—be perceived. God will never respond to cries for mercy and prayers of desperation again. The Word tells us that currently God is being patient with us so that we will repent. He answers even the prayers of those who do not know Him. After His final return, those who did not confess Him before will never see Him again. They will not even be able to speak to Him. It will be total separation from God's grace, mercy and love, forever.

We really take for granted how much this really means. Even those who are the furthest distance imaginable from Christ right now cannot fully deny that they recognize some glimmer of God's character and love in creation—in our world. Love had to come from somewhere. Kindness must have an origin. Mercy is something that originated outside of us. These qualities, these concepts and philosophies are something that we all are familiar with, no matter our history and belief system. And with only a brief moment of honest reflection, we can conclude that these things cannot originate with us. We are not the creators of them. It is God alone who is the sole Origin of all that is good. Separation from God means separation from all we hold dear and everything that is good.

- Chapter 11 -

Head in the Clouds ~ Feet on the Ground

"Divorced from logic, reliance on feeling is dangerous,

just as dangerous as logic divorced from love."

-Matthew Dickerson

- Chapter 11 -

Head in the Clouds ~ Feet on the Ground

During the 1960's and 70's there was a widespread movement that took place—the Jesus Movement. Many "Jesus" community groups sprang from this, one of which was called the "Jesus People, USA" and is considered to have been one of the largest. Here is an excerpt from an article I found recently:

> Steve Rabey wrote about this group in *Christianity Today* almost twenty years ago, noting that those involved "...have given up the American dreams of houses, possessions, and bank accounts" (53). What appeared at that time to be "...an intervention of God in

a culture that had been largely written off by society…" (54), is now being viewed as an unhealthy and damaging organization.

-Nancy N.[32]

I've heard from those who lived through this era that many were abandoning their jobs and even daily responsibilities because Jesus could come back at any moment and so nothing mattered anymore. People were just waiting around for Jesus to return and not doing anything productive with their lives. This was both foolish and completely unbiblical and, I believe, due to a simple misinterpretation of Scripture. Though somewhat of a faded trend, there are still those who may think this way, even if much more subtly and apprehensively than those back in the bell-bottom days.

Though those who buy into this philosophy may mean well, good intentions and feeling-based motivations are never enough to substantiate an accurate faith declaration and lifestyle. It is unfortunate that we so often fall prey to living by emotion while neglecting solid truth. Many times truth will contradict our very emotions. It often demands that we actually die to what "feels good" to us so that we can truly find ourselves— in losing ourselves. Sounds complicated, but it's really quite simple.

> "If anyone would come after me, he must deny himself and take up his cross and follow me. For whoever wants to save his life will lose it, but whoever loses his life for me and for the gospel will save it."
>
> -Luke 9:23-24 (NIV)

It would be far too easy to misunderstand what is being said here in this Scripture, as many, not excluding myself, have done. For it depends solely on the way one interprets the Bible. If one were to pluck this one verse—as with many popular verses of the Bible—out of context, letting it stand all by itself and attempting to understand it completely from that singular standpoint, the conclusion would easily be skewed and stretched out of its true purpose and meaning.

When Scripture is taken as a whole, as it should be, we are then able to understand what is being communicated—the heart of it all—on a whole new level. This is a level of understanding that is often completely neglected and seemingly non-existent until we take the trek into deeper truth. Like an man who's heart is filled with enchantment of a foreign land, and what he thinks to understand about it, when one day he travels there and stays for a while, coming to the realization that he in fact new it very little. Petty speculation can only take a person so far, and possibly in the wrong direction.

It isn't until the academic *and* experiential learning are combined that holistic understanding ensues.

What I am talking about here is just this: regarding certain things mentioned in the Scripture about losing oneself to follow Christ, many could interpret it as giving up everything you have: job, money, home, possessions and responsibilities. As we've just discussed, this conclusion would merely be the result of a limited view, and ultimately, a lazy one. Those who would interpret it this way are not taking the time to really understand Scripture as a whole—a body compiled of different parts, each complimenting and relying upon the others. One of the most crucial things I learned in Bible College is this: Scripture cannot ever contradict itself. And the Holy Spirit will never tell us something, or tell us to *do* something that is in direct contradiction to the Word of God.

It isn't until we view Scriptures like these in the light of the entire Bible that we can understand what they mean. In fact, if one were to view this Scripture in the entirety of the whole Bible, they would soon find many Scriptures actually admonishing us to be excellent workers, diligent in our trade. In honoring those over us, we are actually honoring God. (1 Peter 2:13-17) Jesus tells us parables about those who are good stewards of what they've been given, how this is something He completely supports, and actually *requires*. Recall the famous story about the Talents:

"Again, it will be like a man going on a journey, who called his servants and entrusted his wealth to them. To one he gave five bags of gold, to another two bags, and to another one bag, each according to his ability. Then he went on his journey. The man who had received five bags of gold went at once and put his money to work and gained five bags more. So also, the one with two bags of gold gained two more. But the man who had received one bag went off, dug a hole in the ground and hid his master's money. "After a long time the master of those servants returned and settled accounts with them. The man who had received five bags of gold brought the other five. 'Master,' he said, 'you entrusted me with five bags of gold. See, I have gained five more.' "His master replied, '**Well done, good and faithful servant!** You have been faithful with a few things; I will put you in charge of many things. Come and share your master's happiness!' "The man with two bags of gold also came. 'Master,' he said, 'you entrusted me with two bags of gold; see, I have gained two more.' "His master replied, '**Well done, good and faithful servant!** You have been faithful with a few things; I will put you in charge of many things. Come and share your master's happiness!' "Then the man who had received one bag of gold came. 'Master,' he said, 'I knew that you are a hard man,

> harvesting where you have not sown and gathering where you have not scattered seed. [25] So I was afraid and went out and hid your gold in the ground. See, here is what belongs to you.' "His master replied, '**You wicked, lazy servant**! So you knew that I harvest where I have not sown and gather where I have not scattered seed? Well then, you should have put my money on deposit with the bankers, so that when I returned I would have received it back with interest. "'So take the bag of gold from him and give it to the one who has ten bags. For whoever has will be given more, and they will have an abundance. Whoever does not have, even what they have will be taken from them. And throw that worthless servant outside, into the darkness, where there will be weeping and gnashing of teeth.'
>
> -Matthew 25:14-30 (NIV)

As is made quite clear in this section of Scripture, God is adamant about us being good stewards with our "talents". And what is a "talent" specifically? You may wonder, "How does this apply to me?" Let's take a closer look at meaning of the word "talent" as it was meant to be understood when this Scripture was first penned. The Greek word that is used here is ταλαντον. It is transliterated into English as "talanton". The original meaning of the word is as follows:

> **τάλαντον talanton**; from a prim. root; *a balance,* hence *that which is weighed,* i.e. *a talent* (about 3000 shekels in weight.[33]

Thus, it is fairly obvious that the word "talent" is mainly referring to monetary wealth. This is the primary message: God cares about how we invest monetary wealth. Of course, this can be applied to other areas as well—not just finances—and would in fact not contradict Scripture as a whole, obviously. But I think it is vital to grasp here that God does in fact want us to be wise with our money. This of course means working hard, holding down an occupation that produces revenue and investing what is earned instead of burying it in hopes it will grow all on its own, magically. If the "Jesus People" of the hippie era would have looked a little closer into what the Bible actually had to say, they could have saved themselves a lot of painful consequences due to misunderstanding.

End-Time Addicts

Some people like to play the game of "How would you rather die." Others simply contemplate this in their own heads, not confiding their conclusion to anyone, or the fact that they are thinking so morbidly. And though the former may "only be joking around, having a laugh", from a serious contemplative standpoint, this is nonsense, not to mention a waste of time.

The truth is, we have no idea how it will happen. That is not a choice left up to us, in the *natural* flow of things that is. Of course someone can take their own life if they so choose, but that does not count. It is not playing by the rules and is not fair. And besides, that is not at all what I am referring to here. What I am talking about is solely how people die without deliberately doing it themselves: unexpectedly. This either happens by slowly aging out of this world or sudden accidents or illness.

Ultimately, no one really knows when or how it will happen, but inevitably it will. That much we know for sure. Unless of course God decides to take you up to Him like Enoch (Genesis 5:24) or Elijah (2 Kings 2:11-12)—as the story goes in the Old Testament—so as to never taste death. But then again, this too would come as a complete surprise. Focusing too much on this question of how and when is once again looking at the wrong issue entirely. It is unnecessary and doesn't do anyone any good whatsoever. It is merely a distraction from what we should be giving our attention to.

As we all know deep down, to live life to the fullest and make the most of each day we have on earth should be the center of our focus. That is what will do the most good for us, and those around us. Likewise, we shouldn't worry so much about what heaven will be like or how we can get there any faster. We must keep it in mind of course and look forward to the ultimately inexplicable glory that awaits us there as believers. But to spend all our time mulling over end-time prophecies and descriptions of St. Peter waiting at the Pearly Gates is simply not productive.

Far too easy it is to spend our energies and affections on the world to come, only to the neglect of the world we live in today, missing the herein for the sake of the hereafter. In doing this, we fail to realize a simple yet vital truth: the herein comes before the hereafter. It is therefore more pertinent an issue to address presently, that is of course, in the light of the hope of heaven. Living in the light of eternity should actually bring illumination to our current path here on earth, not distort our vision of it by getting caught up in fanciful visions and dreams.

Don't get me wrong here. I am not at all opposed to visions of heaven; after all, I did just write an entire chapter on it (The Great Beyond: The Glorious Shore). My purpose in addressing this issue in greater detail is simply to bring a healthy balance. I have seen people who get so obsessed with end-time prophecies and visions of heaven—and the pursuit of such—who end up actually neglecting their daily responsibilities, and skewing their Biblical understanding by getting so caught up in the "supernatural". And though I support supernatural occurrences and dynamic visions that are "out of this world", I also have come to a place where I perceive the supernatural invading every single day and area of my life. I perceive the miraculous work of God in the way He transforms lives, as well as in cleaning up my own house; I see His hand at work when He puts it on someone's heart to bless me with a large sum of money, and yet I also recognize His work in a simple encouraging—or convicting—word that proceeds from the mouth of a friend, or family member. I acknowledge His divine hand in physical healings, and in the same breath see His otherworldly power working through me when I choose to "turn the other cheek" upon being wronged.

"Glory" Chasers

Moments when heaven invades earth are not limited to the far and between occurrences of tangibly dynamic spiritual experiences. Those who spend all of their time chasing after signs and wonders and the next spiritual high, are not truly concerned with the heart and character God would like to instill into their lives, but rather, they are ultimately preoccupied and caught up in the emotional high that makes them feel so good. And though this motivation isn't entirely wrong, and can actually be used for good when kept in balance, it usually ends up causing those who apply it too heavily to neglect a more solidified understanding of God in exchange for the goose bumps they get. This, I believe, was the demise of the "Jesus People". They had ended up defining their own terms of belief and a warped perspective of true biblical Christianity, due to shallow interpretation of Scripture.

I feel the need to reiterate yet again: I am not at all opposed to the more tangible supernatural experiences and I myself am one who longs to see more of God's visible power at work in our world. I know many who share this passionate desire and yet their lives, like my own, are orderly. I simply mean that we share a common belief that holding down a job, paying bills, taking care of basic needs and wisely managing resources are of high importance to God, and thus, should be to us as well. As a matter of fact, it is truth that when someone really comes to know what God is like—through rightly reading the Word of God—they actually become better at their profession and managing their duties. It is the converse of what seemed to be the effect of following Christ in the case of the "Jesus People".

One of the biggest problems with relying too much on feelings, signs and wonders—as well as sitting around waiting for Jesus to return neglecting the responsible life He calls us to live—is that it produces no fruit. As the saying goes, "Fruit grows in the valley, not the mountaintop." Therefore, though mountaintop experiences are both beneficial and can be life changing, the change will only last—will only bear fruit—if one carries the mountaintop experience with them into the valley. They are moments for us to refresh and re-gather our focus and strength, but we cannot stay on the mountain. We must descend back into the valley—our everyday responsibilities and relationships—and bear fruit. Though we may be looking directly upon Jesus Christ with affection and gratitude, we will quickly fall away when trials come if we don't develop a more solid understanding of who He is and what *He* would have us do. Otherwise, we will come to find we have not been standing upon solid truth, but rather have been holding up our own finite definitions and beliefs—mingled with our own opinions and preferences—which will easily crumble to bits as soon as pressure is applied.

Angel Dust

Another example of theology gone awry is the account of the Lakeland, FL revival that was led by Todd Bentley in recent years. I once attended one of his meetings that was held in the NW a while back and will admit much of it was in fact biblical. He spoke a lot about biblical healing, signs and wonders and so on. At the very worst, I simply thought it odd that he spent so much time talking about donating to his ministry. Today, however, there is much more that has been revealed about this man's ministry and how it went wrong that causes me to be extra cautious about such movements (revivals).

I remember sitting in one of my Bible college classes and hearing the professor share about the details of the Lakeland Revival and how it was becoming strange. People were claiming to have had very descriptive encounters with angels: seeing feathers, gold dust and jewels falling on them during worship. One man even claimed on the platform to have been operated on by an angel. Here is an excerpt from an article I came across on the Charisma:

> "During the Lakeland Revival last year in Florida, a man from Germany took the stage and claimed that an angel walked into a restaurant while he was eating a hamburger, took his intestines out and replaced them with a gold substance. Others have testified that angels took them to heaven and operated on them. And many are claiming that angels are dropping feathers, gold dust and precious gems on worshippers."
>
> -J. Lee Grady[34]

There are also accounts of Bentley punching a man with cancer as a form of "laying on of hands"—which is not by a long shot a solitary instance. I realize that some enthusiasts of violent faith in God's miraculous healing like that of Smith Wigglesworth—of whom I'm certain Bentley was an avid admirer—would not actually be entirely surprised by this. Even if at first it seems shocking, the thought of a man of God doing similar things back in the early 1900's soothes the question of legitimacy. For example, there is the story of Wigglesworth drop-kicking a dead baby across a hospital room that then returned to life. Whether this story is actually true is yet unknown. Many Christians immediately buy into it, however, as completely of God. For me, it doesn't completely add up. To think that just because it worked is reason enough to form a theology around it is ludicrous! I can't think of a single instance in Scripture where anything remotely similar happened. Actually, I see quite the opposite in the way Jesus healed people. He was gentle, though controversial, and would never have pulled back to deck someone or give them the boot in order to heal them. This was not the way He demonstrated His power. The question then arises regarding instances like that with Wigglesorth: was it of God? Possibly. But then again, maybe not. (That is to say of course that the account is valid.) Even if God did bring the baby back to life, and heal the man Bentley punched in the gut, that doesn't at all mean that He approved of such behavior. In my humble opinion, if it's not in the Bible, it doesn't belong in our theology.

A section of Scripture comes to mind in contemplating this issue. It is the story of when Moses was told by God to *speak* to the rock in the wilderness so that water would come forth for the people, and Moses struck it instead, twice. And though the water God had promised still flowed forth from the rock, God specifically told Moses that because of his disobedience in this matter, he would never enter the Promise Land. This is certainly something to ponder.

> The LORD said to Moses, Take the staff, and you and your brother Aaron gather the assembly together. **Speak** to that rock before their eyes and it will pour out its water. You will bring water out of the rock for the community so that they and their livestock can drink. So Moses took the staff from the LORD's presence, just as he commanded him. He and Aaron gathered the assembly together in front of the rock and Moses said to them, Listen, you rebels, must we bring you water out of this rock? Then Moses raised his arm and **struck** the rock twice with his staff. Water gushed out, and the community and their livestock drank. *But the LORD said to Moses and Aaron, Because you did not trust in me enough to honor me as holy in the sight of the Israelites, you will not bring this community into the land I give them.*
>
> -Numbers 20:7-12 (NIV; *italics and emphasis mine*)

And what was the outcome of the revival Bentley led? Well, it ultimately fell apart. For it was recently found out that he was having an affair with a member of his ministry. He ended up divorcing his wife and marrying the woman with whom he committed adultery. It seems that Matthew 7:20—a Scripture

Bentley often quoted in support of his ministry—has instead exposed wrong thinking and poor character, and all in exchange for the "glory". Simply put, "...you will know them by their fruits." (NASB)

Summing It Up

I'm sure you've at one time or another received one of those fancy flyers printed on glossy cardstock hailing titles of epic proportions in the mail. You know, the ones inviting you to some sort of conference about the end of the world, interpreting the signs of the times through the book of Revelation, and so on and so forth. I must admit that I have quite the disdain for propaganda such as this. The reason being, it is a waste of time. God did not intend for us to sit around discussing how and when the world was going to end. It is not His desire for us to make endless comparisons between violence portrayed in the book of Revelation and what is happening in Iraq. He does not think it productive of us to be staring up into the sky, trying to figure out when He will return.

I'm sure you've heard about the recent events in which a

man named Harold Camping claimed to have deciphered the exact date and time that Jesus would return via mathematical calculations in Scripture. It was all over the news. Apparently, this was his second prediction—actually it was his third; he had also made a prediction back in 2004 but later recanted that saying he made a mathematical error. He made amends for his second mistake by claiming that the earlier date was simply the Rapture, and only Jesus knows who was taken. Here is an excerpt from an ABC News article that was taken from Camping's website:

> Thus we can be sure that the whole world, with the exception of those who are presently saved (the elect), are under the judgment of God, and will be annihilated together with the whole physical world on October 21, 2011, on the last day of the present five months period," it says. "On that day the true believers (the elect) will be raptured. We must remember that only God knows who His elect are that He saved prior to May 21."[35]

What amazes and frustrates me most about this statement of his, is that he claims himself to be a Christian. The obvious question is this: how could someone so publicly pronounced to be associated with the name of Christ be so ignorant to His teachings?

There were even giant billboards made advertising this campaign and proclaiming in a shiny gold seal, " The Bible Guarantees It."[36] And he wasn't the only one to believe this! Apparently Camping had amassed quite the following from his bold declaration—many of which are not too happy about the whole fiasco now. These people—mostly Christians—fervently believed everything about this "mathematical" discovery and spent time storming the streets with picket signs proclaiming their Doomsday message.

What is really sad about this—aside from the fact that the world didn't end of course—is that this man led all these people astray by getting so caught up in high and mighty predictions, losing sight of the most simple and crucial biblical truths. How someone who claimed to be a Bible scholar, or a Christian at all, could miss such an obvious section of Scripture as the following is beyond me:

> "So if anyone tells you, 'There he is, out in the wilderness,' do not go out; or, 'Here he is, in the inner rooms,' **do not believe it**. For as lightning that comes from the east is visible even in the west, so will be the coming of the Son of Man…"**But about that day or hour no one knows**, not even the angels in heaven, nor the Son, but only the Father. As it was in the days of

> Noah, so it will be at the coming of the Son of Man. For in the days before the flood, people were eating and drinking, marrying and giving in marriage, up to the day Noah entered the ark; and they knew nothing about what would happen until the flood came and took them all away. That is how it will be at the coming of the Son of Man. Two men will be in the field; one will be taken and the other left. Two women will be grinding with a hand mill; one will be taken and the other left. "*Therefore keep watch*, because you do not know on what day your Lord will come. But understand this: If the owner of the house had known at what time of night the thief was coming, he would have kept watch and would not have let his house be broken into. So you also must be ready, because the Son of Man will come at an hour when you do not expect him."
>
> -Matthew 24:26-7, 36-44 (NIV)

It would seem that anyone who followed this false prophecy—including Camping firstly of course—would have had to either never read their Bible, or simply torn the page out upon which this section of Scripture rests.

Not only do these types of careless exegesis result in leading others astray, further unnecessary ridicule ensues as well. And this kind of ridicule is not the type that God Himself defends us against. It is not as if someone simply stood up for their belief in Christ and is thus being persecuted for it. No, this public shame is a direct representation of the kind of Christianity the world runs away from: good old fashioned fire and brimstone, soap box, street corner preaching that leaves people jeering from an absolute careless concern for others—all righteous zeal and no deep level of love.

You'll note in the Scripture quotation above, I have italicized the phrase "therefore keep watch." This strikes an interesting chord doesn't it? Especially after all that talk I just gave about not staring into the sky looking for Jesus to return instead of taking care of our lives. Much like many sections of Scripture that sometimes seem to contradict themselves, this does in fact make sense. But it requires stretching our thinking. Here, God is not telling us to keep watch by the most obvious sense of staring into the wild blue yonder waiting for the sky to fall on us. He is rather telling us to live our lives in a way that is keeping watch—or better yet, readying ourselves for His return: His completely unexpected and unpredictable return. Let's open up the Scriptures some more and look at the context.

> "Who then is the faithful and wise servant, whom the master has put in charge of the servants in his household

> to give them their food at the proper time? **It will be good for that servant whose master finds him doing so when he returns**. Truly I tell you, he will put him in charge of all his possessions."
>
> -Matthew 24:45-47 (NIV; *emphasis mine*)

Here we see clearly that what Christ means by "keeping watch" is simply living responsibly and obedient to the tasks He sets before us. Instead of being consumed with predictions of the future and the end of the world, we should simply live each day to the fullest of its potential in His will. Those who spend all their time, resources and energy on chasing these other flights of fancy would do well to take heed to the following piece of Scripture:

> "They were looking intently up into the sky as he was going, when suddenly two men dressed in white stood beside them. "Men of Galilee," they said, "why do you stand here looking into the sky? This same Jesus, who has been taken from you into heaven, will come back in the same way you have seen him go into heaven."
>
> -Acts 1:10-11 (NIV)

And what the angels meant by, "…in the same way you have seen Him go into heaven" is simply this: completely unexpected, but certainly not unnoticed.

- Chapter 12 -

The King and His Kingdom

"God will invade. But I wonder whether people who ask God to interfere openly and directly in our world quite realise what it will be like when He does. When that happens, it is the end of the world. When the author walks on to the stage the play is over. God is going to invade, all right: but what is the good of saying you are on His side then, when you see the whole natural universe melting away like a dream and something else - something it never entered your head to conceive - comes crashing in; something so beautiful to some of us and so terrible to others that none of us will have any choice left? For this time it will be God without disguise; something so overwhelming that it will strike either irresistible love or irresistible horror into every creature. It will be too late then to choose your side… it will be the time when we discover which side we really have chosen, whether we realised it before or not."

-C.S. Lewis[37]

- Chapter 12 -

The King and His Kingdom

The word Kingdom is a well-known concept in the Bible, as well as in the world at large. The reality of what the Kingdom of God is, and the King who reigns over it, are however, shrouded by much mystery. Like any other area of faith, this requires some extended level of research to more fully understand. At first glance, the words Kingdom and King very likely mean to us something entirely different from the way God would define them. And when brought face to face with the truest definition, we have a choice to make, much like the Pharisees and teachers of the Law in Jesus' days on earth. They did not have open minds toward God's true King and Kingdom, and thus, when the King appeared, declaring the true message about the Kingdom of God, they refused to believe it. They had formed their own ideas—even a culture if you will—around what they believed the promised Messiah would be like, and what kind of kingdom He would establish on earth. They were ultimately caught off guard.

> "Jesus was not the rescuing, redeeming, oppression-beating king that the Pharisees expected. Jesus did not fit the 'opinion mould' that they had formed, therefore, in their eyes, he was not the Messiah."
>
> -Rick McNamara[38]

God has never been confined to the tiny classifications and ideas we make about Him. Even when He constricted Himself within fragile human frame, we still see His glory bursting the seams of this man who faced the religious leaders of those days with such bold authority and heavenly proclamations. Jesus came proclaiming a Kingdom all right, but not at all what they had expected or hoped for. The problem was they were more concerned with the natural world and things as they saw them than the supernatural, the heavenly, and most of all, the humble. The Scripture is true of them that says, "…knowledge puffs up…" (1 Corinthians 8:1; NIV)

A Humble King

The things that Jesus was concerned about stood in complete contradiction to what the Pharisees and religious leaders believed their Coming King would be about. And one of the most substantial differences we see in their point of view and character from that of Christ, was something called humility. As stated previously, they had been hoping for a King who would rise to power and Lord that power over the nation, a King that would literally overpower the oppressive government of which they were subject to, and deliver them from political slavery. The concept of a humble servant King, who would tolerate ridicule and shame, and identify with prostitutes and beggars, was so foreign to them that they refused—even violently—His leadership when He came to them.

Even Jesus' own disciples had a difficult time with this, as the expectation of a King who would restore Israel to its former beauty and power permeated the entire culture of the day. It wasn't only limited to the religious leaders. The difference between those who followed Jesus and those who didn't was simply that they were willing to be corrected and learn the truth about God's intentions. This is what set them apart: they cared more about the truth than about popular opinion. The following Scripture is a beautiful example of how Jesus challenged the popular view of leadership:

> A dispute also arose among them as to which of them was considered to be greatest. Jesus said to them, "The kings of the Gentiles lord it over them; and those who exercise authority over them call themselves Benefactors. **But you are not to be like that.** Instead, the greatest among you should be like the youngest, and the one who rules like the one who serves. For who is greater, the one who is at the table or the one who serves? Is it not the one who is at the table? But I am among you as one who serves. You are those who have stood by me in my trials. And I confer on you a kingdom, just as my Father conferred one on me, so that you may eat and drink at my table in my kingdom and sit on thrones, judging the twelve tribes of Israel.
>
> -Luke 22:24-30 (NIV; *emphasis mine*)

One of the most remarkable elements of this statement Jesus makes is the context in which it sits. If we look at the account that John gave of the Last Supper, as it shows a little more than Luke's, we see that Jesus had just finished washing His disciples' feet—all of them. This includes Judas, whom Jesus already knew was going to betray Him. Washing feet was a duty that only the lowliest of servants would fulfill; yet Jesus, the King of kings and Lord of lords did it without hesitation. Thus He displayed what kind of King He is, and what kind of Kingdom He rules over.

> "The evening meal was in progress, and the devil had already prompted Judas, the son of Simon Iscariot, to betray Jesus. Jesus knew that the Father had put all things under his power, and that he had come from God and was returning to God; so he got up from the meal, took off his outer clothing, and wrapped a towel around his waist. **After that, he poured water into a basin and began to wash his disciples' feet**, drying them with the towel that was wrapped around him."
>
> -John 13:2-5 (NIV; *emphasis mine*)

This act took the disciples completely by surprise, especially Peter, as we see in his response to Jesus washing his feet only a moment later. It was not at all what they would expect a "king" to do. And why would they? The world has always portrayed kings as high and mighty, always with an air of fanfare and pomp. Never would it be considered noble in the eyes of their society for a king to stoop this low, performing the duties of the lowest servant. This would have not only seemed ridiculous, it would have been offensive and even considered unsightly to many.

By coming as a "humble King", Jesus showed what kind of conquering He was really about to do. He did in fact come to overthrow oppressive government and society; He did intend to do away with the tyrannical reign that enslaved His people. However, this overthrowing as it were, would not be accomplished from an external standpoint; rather, Jesus was aiming at the heart of the issue. He had come to overthrow the most destructive tyrant enslaving all mankind—pride.

After all, didn't we establish in earlier chapters that the plight of mankind, which was firstly the demise of Lucifer, was pride? It is in that cancer—that sinful infection—of self-promotion and ruling whatever authority you have over others, that the most destructive oppressor is found. The Pharisees, teachers of the law, and even Jesus' own disciples may have thought that their worst enemy was the government of their day, but King Jesus graciously came to show them, and us, the error in that way of thinking. By His words and His actions we see God communicating that the oppressive government most in need of conquering is within ourselves. It is our own pride.

Fortunately, Jesus' closest disciples eventually allowed God to change their thinking and transform them completely. Yet, as is very unfortunate, many who witnessed a direct display and declaration of the true nature of God's Kingship, refused to overcome their own pride. They chose rather to hold on to preconceived ideals of a king, an expectation that was false and thus left them in a permanent state of disappointment.

A Different Kind of Kingdom

> "Are we concentrating more on the kingdom of this world than on the kingdom that is not of this world?"
>
> -Philip Yancey[39]

Like every other area we have discussed so far, in order to understand the concept of the Kingdom of God—in its truest form—we must look outside of our own understanding, beyond the confines of this world, this so-called reality. We see this clearly in the way Jesus responded to Pilate when asked to explain His kingship:

> Jesus said, "My kingdom is not of this world. If it were, my servants would fight to prevent my arrest by the Jewish leaders. But now my kingdom is from another place."
>
> -John 18:36 (NIV)

Jesus said that His Kingdom is "not of this world" and that it is "from another place". How could we ever expect to interpret its true nature by looking at the way things work in the world? This will not do. We must allow our minds to be opened to a greater reality; a reality that often completely contradicts what we would think a kingdom should be like. The requirement is the same today as it was two thousand years ago. God is still challenging the status quo. After all, He is the same yesterday, today and forever; He never changes (Hebrews 13:8), and in that case, it is only we who are to change.

What I find is that far too often when we attempt to understand certain things about the Kingdom of God, we do so from a limited perspective. Not that that is a bad thing necessarily. It is more an issue when the limitedness of our view is coupled with stubbornness, or closed-mindedness. What occurs most often in these types of scenarios is that we are simply asking the wrong questions, rather, questions that do not matter near as much as we think they do. Take for example the following Scripture, when the disciples were asking Jesus about His Kingdom.

> Then they gathered around him and asked him, "Lord, are you at this time going to restore the kingdom to Israel?" He said to them: "It is not for you to know the times or dates the Father has set by his own authority."
>
> -Acts 1:6-7 (NIV)

What happens next is almost humorous; Jesus changes the subject immediately! He turns His disciples' attention back to what He really wants to tell them, like a teacher directing the wandering eyes of an ADD inflicted youngster back to the front of the classroom. For in the very next verse, this is what Jesus says:

> "But you will receive power when the Holy Spirit comes on you; and you will be my witnesses in Jerusalem, and in all Judea and Samaria, and to the ends of the earth."
>
> -Acts 1:8 (NIV)

In effect, what He is saying is, "Pay attention! Let go of your pre-conceived notions about my Kingdom and how it affects you, and let me show you what it really is like." What is His Kingdom like then? From what we can see here, it is about being Christ's "witnesses" in the world by the power of God that is given by the Holy Spirit. That is what Kingdom living looks like: people living in close relationship with the King, receiving His authority and power, and then reaching the world with His true Kingdom message—a message of overcoming selfish pride and loving others; a message that isn't received well by the stiff-necked and religiously pious.

Another profound thought we see while looking deeper into this particular Scripture, is how Jesus is basically saying the Kingdom of God is not just something that will be around us, or merely affect us externally, rather it is actually something that will be within us. The question His disciples asked was when Jesus would restore the Kingdom of Israel. Jesus in a way changes the subject but He also answers their question in an unexpected way when He says, "But you will receive power when the Holy Spirit comes upon you." The power of the Kingdom of God, which they hoped for, would come in a way they didn't expect. It would not come beginning with outward authority and power, but rather inward.

> Once, having been asked by the Pharisees when the kingdom of God would come, Jesus replied, The kingdom of God does not come with your careful observation, nor will people say, 'Here it is,' or 'There it is,' **because the kingdom of God is within you.**
>
> -Luke 17:20-21 (NIV; *emphasis mine*)

Again, the first and most important area of God's reign is inside of us. God is not nearly as concerned about the external as He is with the internal (Matthew 23:27). Once the inside is under the rule of Christ, all other areas of life follow suit. Furthermore, even if the entire world around us were in absolute rebellion of God's Kingdom, we as His royal heirs would still walk in a power and authority not of this world. The world cannot lay claim to any area of our lives if the Kingdom we are part of is from "another place" as Jesus said. This may merely be something we have not yet fully realized.

And what happens when the inner self (the real "us" as seen in chapter 2: The Unseen You) is an active member of the Kingdom of God and subject to the Ruler of that Kingdom? Once again, all we really must do is reflect on who Jesus is—who He showed Himself to be—as we discussed only a moment ago. He is the humble King, willing to lower Himself and serve others in ways that no one would ever expect a King to do. His motivation was always love for His people and wanting to be near to them. And most of all, He was even willing to die for His own people, who were all of them unfaithful to Him, so that He could be near to them. For we all know that our sin separates us from God. The only chance for reunion was that the price of death was paid, which Jesus did with His own blood.

Have you ever heard of a king who was willing to give His own life and take all the blame for a people who had only spat in his face time and again? It is completely different than the way we, as fallen human beings, would naturally think. We would say a king would be about justice! If a people did wrong, then they should be punished! Of course we would not say this about ourselves, but about some other poor wretch. And there again, we see our pride rearing its ugly head, and we begin to perceive the need for a Kingdom not ruled by the ideals and philosophies of the world around us. Were it left to us, the idea of the King himself dying for the people and paying their penalty of death—taking their condemnation upon himself even when he did no wrong—would be the furthest from our minds.

I realize that there are many other descriptions about the Kingdom of God in the Bible, most of them given by Jesus Himself in parables. I do not wish to expound upon all of these, as there are merely some specific—and more pertinent—points I wanted to make about what God's Kingdom is like, and what kind of subjects we are to be within that Kingdom. I will, however, explore one of these parables here.

The Parable of the Pearl

"Again, the kingdom of heaven is like a merchant
looking for fine pearls.
When he found one of great value,
he went away and sold everything he had and bought it."
-Matthew 13:45-46 (NIV)

This parable, though one of the shortest that Jesus ever told, is quite profound. Have you ever found something, or someone, you were willing to give everything up for? That no matter how much wealth, knowledge or possessions you amassed in life, you would sell them all just to have that one thing, or be with that one person?

It could be a dream job, it could be a family; maybe it's a person you love, or a country you desire to live in. There comes a time in everyone's life when they find something that is of greater value than everything else they've ever seen. Sometimes this is later on, when one grows old, and occasionally it happens sooner. What is the one thing, or person, you would give everything up for, if you had to? If you knew there was no way you could have it while still holding on to what you had. If you came to the realization that you would have to "sell" what you had in order to buy a thing of far greater value to you, would you not do whatever was required? What is your "pearl" of greatest value?

For me, it is my relationship with Christ—a relationship that has its origins in a radical transformation that occurred nearly ten years ago. At that time, I realized that everything I had accumulated in my life—everything that I thought was valuable—was really trash compared with the near-blinding shine of this "pearl" I had discovered, this proposition from God to bring me into a Kingdom of light, a Kingdom of heaven. At that moment, I chose to "sell" everything I had to get that "pearl".

This, I believe, is really the heart of what Jesus is communicating regarding the Kingdom of heaven. He is illustrating in a beautifully simple and artistic way what it is like when someone enters His Kingdom. It is easy for us to think that we have such valuable things in our lives, until the time when we find the "pearl" of greater value than anything else, and suddenly all our possessions, ideas, opinions and preferences seem worthless in comparison. And it's not even a fair trade! The Bible says that the man "sold" everything he had to buy the pearl. God chooses to give us that "pearl" in exchange for things that are of no comparable value. It's not because He needs these things; rather, it is because we need to give them up. We cannot hold so tightly to what we have and expect to receive what God wants to give us. It is in surrendering ourselves that we find the greatest treasure. We must lose our life in order to find it; we must "sell" it all to buy the "pearl".

This is what the "religious" of Jesus' day failed to realize. They held so tightly to their traditions, ideals, possessions—and most of all, their pride—that even when the "pearl" appeared to them, their vision was blurred, their minds were closed, and they refused to look upon its beauty. Thus, they never perceived how insignificant everything else was when held up to the true Kingdom of God. For there is only one price we must pay to enter the Kingdom, and it is really the only price we have the ability to pay. That price is simply our very own lives, surrendered to a King who does not lord His authority over us as we might expect Him to. Rather, this King desires to serve us, even to wash our feet. That is what He requires of us, that we would go and do the same. (John 13:15) This is what the true King, and His Kingdom, is like.

- CHAPTER 13 -

THE HOUSE

"I love Thy kingdom, Lord,
The house of Thine abode,
The church our blessed Redeemer saved
With His own precious blood."

-Timothy Dwight

- Chapter 13 -

The House

Ἐκκλησία is the Greek word from which we get the English word "Church". It is transliterated as "ekklēsia". If we are talking about the Kingdom of God, how on earth could we not mention the Church? For it is such an essential part of what God is doing in establishing His Kingdom. Jesus used this word when He told Peter His intentions for His Kingdom people:

> "And I tell you that you are Peter, and on this rock I will build my **church** [ekklēsia], and the gates of Hades will not overcome it."
>
> -Matthew 16:18 (NIV; *emphasis mine*)

Contrary to what many may believe about the word church, and where it originates, it does not mean “a physical building”. And even those who know very well that this word does not mean simply a building, would do well to remind themselves of this truth continually—myself included. For when one loses sight of this truth for even an instant, falling prey to complacency of faith would become far too easy. If someone thinks that being a part of the Church is merely attending faithfully every Sunday service—and whatever other services are held at a particular church building throughout the week—that person would be gravely mistaken. That is not at all what the Bible teaches.

This word “ekklēsia” literally means “assembly” or “a gathering of people”[40] and was used by the culture of Jesus’ day in accordance with that very meaning. This word is never used in the New Testament as a “building”. In using this word to describe what His desires for His people were on earth, and what kind of Kingdom He was beginning to establish, He used a word that I’m sure would have been very clear and understandable to His listeners. This is yet another reason why proper biblical interpretation is so vital, for we are in fact hearing a message originally intended for an ancient audience, and as such, we must listen through their ears. We must put ourselves in their shoes.

Jesus did not come to build glorious church buildings with towering steeples and stain-glass windows. What He wants to build is an "assembly" of believers. His desire is that we would be a community constantly gathering together in prayer, fellowship and worship. A building is simply a place where that can be done more effectively. But how could we dare to ever dub an earthly building as more holy than the people of God gathering within it! It is not the mud and clay, bricks and mortar which are sanctified—after all, inanimate objects with no life. No, it is us, the people of God's Kingdom gathered together—wherever that may be—in unity, love and thankfulness to God that should be considered a holy thing. Man makes buildings, and thus they are temporal; God made us in His image and likeness, putting His very breath within us, and thus, we are eternal.

SECTION ONE: Oikos

There is another word in Scripture that talks about the assembly of God's people (church); that word is "house". When we take a closer look at this word alongside the previous one, we see a beautiful and fuller picture of God's dwelling among us, and working through us, as Kingdom people.

> "Although I hope to come to you soon, I am writing you these instructions so that, if I am delayed, you will know how people ought to conduct themselves in God's **household, which is the church** of the living God, the pillar and foundation of the truth."
>
> -1 Timothy 3:15 (NIV; *emphasis mine*)

Paul, writing instruction to his disciple Timothy, uses the word "house"—more specifically "household"—here to describe what the Church ultimately is. This word "household" comes from the root Greek word οἶκος which is transliterated as "oikos". This word of course means "house" but also can be used as: home, a physical edifice; of royalty; palace; of deity; temple; by extension: family, lineage, people who live in or originated in a particular house.[41] "House of God" and "Temple" are words used to describe the gathering of God's people mainly in the Old Testament, which shows that God's intentions have been the same all along, though now simply amplified and more tangible. And the meaning of all this goes further and deeper still. We ourselves are in fact God's dwelling! He makes His home inside of us. When once we let Him in completely, God actually makes His abode within us! As first Corinthians 3:16 says, "Do you not know that you are a temple of God and that the Spirit of God dwells in you?" (NASB)

This is where it all begins, for without God first indwelling us as individuals, what place do we have in the gathering of God's people? What home would we find in that place without being a home for the Holy Spirit ourselves? By no means am I saying that only believers should be allowed in Christian gatherings. That would be completely against God's heart. God desires that all should come to Him and far too often we, as the Church, get in the way of that desire.

SECTION TWO: Oikodomeō

The righteous will flourish like a palm tree, they will grow like a cedar of Lebanon; planted in the house of the LORD, they will flourish in the courts of our God. They will still bear fruit in old age, they will stay fresh and green, proclaiming, The LORD is upright; he is my Rock, and there is no wickedness in him.

-Psalm 92:12-15 (NIV)

Referring back to Matthew 16:18, which we discussed only a moment ago, there is another very important word I would like to expound upon. This word is similar to the last one we discussed and is used in direct conjunction with it by Jesus in this verse. When coupled with the other two words we have used, it helps to bring us to a much more thorough understanding of the way in which God's Kingdom is tangibly expressed here on earth. As Bill Scheidler once said, "The Church is the visible expression of the Kingdom of God in the earth."

The word that I am referring to is οἰκοδομέω, which is transliterated to "oikodomeō". This word literally means, "build; to build up; rebuild" and more specifically in this instance, "to build a house".[42] This concept is much more significant than we may think at first glance. In the example Scripture I provided of where this word appears, Jesus says, "I will *build* [oikodomeō] my church." He is ultimately saying, "I will build, build up, rebuild [where there has been any falling apart due to neglect of its members]. For we know that He goes on to say the gates of Hades will not overcome it, and therefore can conclude any tearing down of His church would ultimately come from within (see Revelation 2:1).

Furthermore He is saying, "I will build My house, the place where I will dwell with my people". This idea of building bears with it some interesting elements, which we will break down into sections.

The Beauty of Imperfection

Firstly, the thought of Church undergoing a continual building process insinuates that the obvious point that it is not yet finished. This should bring some level of encouragement when one takes a look at the current state of the Church. For anyone can see it is not perfect. As has been said before, "Where there are people, there are problems." Thus, as long as people are flawed—which of course is until Jesus returns and bestows upon us glorified bodies (as addressed in previous chapters)—the Church will also be imperfect.

It doesn't do us any good to fixate on all the blemishes and flaws of the Church, though. This is not something God desires us to be about. I believe that is a direct tactic of the enemy so that we will not be unified as believers. The devil knows that there is power in numbers; that's why he tries to get us alone. When he's got us there, to keep us in a constant state of judging the imperfections of others, staying annoyed and agitated with all their quirks and habits so that we won't care to get any closer to them. I am reminded in this instance of a short segment from C.S. Lewis' theological satire *The Screwtape Letters.*

There is a scene in this book where Screwtape—a demon—is coaching his nephew Wormwood—another demon—regarding his assignment to keep a particular man away from becoming a Christian. In this particular instance it is made known to us that the man has in fact converted to Christianity and Screwtape makes it clear that this is a failure on his nephew's part that will not go without punishment. What comes next, however, is quite interesting; Screwtape begins to tell of another tactic.

> "I note with grave displeasure that your patient has become a Christian. Do not indulge the hope that you will escape the usual penalties; indeed, in your better moments, I trust you would hardly even wish to do so. In the meantime we must make the best of the situation. There is no need to despair; hundreds of these adult converts have been reclaimed after a brief sojourn in the Enemy's camp and are now with us. All the habits of the patient, both mental and bodily, are still in our favour. One of our great allies at present is the Church itself. **Do not misunderstand me**. I do not mean the Church as we see her spread but through all time and space and rooted in eternity, terrible as an army with banners. That, I

confess, is a spectacle which makes our boldest tempters uneasy. But fortunately it is quite invisible to these humans. **All your patient sees is the half-finished, sham Gothic erection on the new building estate.** When he goes inside, he sees the local grocer with rather an oily expression on his face bustling up to offer him one shiny little book containing a liturgy which neither of them understands, and one shabby little book containing corrupt texts of a number of religious lyrics, mostly bad, and in very small print. When he gets to his pew and looks around him he sees just that selection of his neighbors whom he has hitherto avoided. You want to lean pretty heavily on those neighbors. Make his mind flit to and fro between an expression like "the body of Christ" and the actual faces in the next pew. It matters very little, of course, what kind of people that next pew really contains. You may know one of them to be a great warrior on the Enemy's side. No matter. Your patient, thanks to Our Father below, is a fool. **Provided that any of those neighbors sing out of tune, or have boots that squeak, or double chins, or odd clothes, the patient will quite easily believe that their religion must therefore be somehow ridiculous.**"[43]

Though Lewis takes some artistic liberties in this almost humorous satire, there is a very sobering and profound air to what he has written. And I'm sure that almost anyone who's ever been in Church for any amount of time can relate to what is being said, and then some. How easy it is to be distracted—and disgruntled—by the little imperfections of those in the Church, distracted from what matters most: a grace-filled community of those who follow Christ. Even though these complaints against other members are often legitimate, what right do I have to hold any magnifying glass up to their flaws? Were I to take a closer look at myself instead of constantly glaring at others, I would most likely find just as many flaws, if not more, than they. It is encouraging to know, and dwell upon the fact, that God loves us just the way we are, imperfections and all. Of course, as I've stated in previous chapters, He does not want us to stay that way and is continually perfecting us. However, it would do us good to remember what Jesus said about it: He said, "*I* will build my Church." He did not say, "*You* will build My Church." This is an interesting point to ponder.

Living Stones

Another aspect of this building process—the most important of all—is what kind of materials God is using to accomplish this task. Though we touched on the subject a little already, I think this area deserves a little more attention. As we can clearly see in Scripture, and as we've already discussed, God's intent is not to construct a fancy church building and call that His Church. As Scripture says, the Church He is building is made up not of lifeless rocks. It is made of "living stones".

> "As you come to Him, the living stone…you also, like living stones, are being built into a spiritual house to be a holy priesthood…"
>
> -I Peter 2:4-5 (NIV)

God intends to build us as believers—His living stones—into a close-knit community, each member supporting the others, each dependent upon the others. When building a structure, there must not be any spaces between the stones. It is required that all of them fit perfectly together in order for the structure to stand. I am not insinuating that God wants us all involved in every single area of each other's lives; that would be ludicrous, not to mention an invasion of privacy. No, I do not believe that is what God is asking for when He says we are to be the very stones with which He builds His Church. I believe what this means is simply that we need to be in agreement with each other. It means that regardless of our differences—and as long as we share the basic doctrines of the Christian faith—we can work together as a team, realizing how much we actually need each other.

> "The body is a unit, though it is made up of many parts; and though all its parts are many, they form *one* body. So it is with Christ...The eye cannot say to the hand, "I don't need you!" And the head cannot say to the feet, "I don't need you!"...you are the body of Christ, and each one of you is a part of it."
>
> -I Corinthians 12:12; 21, 27 (NIV)

This Scripture states that we, as individual members of the Body of Christ (another name for the Church) are each unique and have a role to play. It tells us that no one is an island unto themselves. It ultimately communicates that regardless of our differences, and possibly even annoyances with each other, we must come together as the "body" we are supposed to be under the authority of Jesus—the Head. It is a wonderful description of how the Church is supposed to function: as a living building made up of people who have chosen to let Christ lead them in loving others. People who have realized that just as a physical body needs all the parts to properly—and fully—function, so also, all the parts of the Body of Christ are necessary to effectively live together and bring others into what God is building.

Separate Rooms

Denominations. This is a curious subject. Why is it that there are so many different church groups in our present day society? Well, I think ultimately it must have to do with disagreements about certain particulars of doctrinal belief and theological chemistry. There are some that preach only love and grace, and others only hellfire and brimstone condemnations shouted from the pulpit. Some church groups pray in tongues and believe that all the Gifts of the Spirit are still alive and active today, while still others frown upon such, as they would say, "heretical" beliefs holding to a proclamation that said Gifts ended after Pentecost.

Though much debate surrounds so many issues of the faith, most of it could be cleared up with a little proper biblical interpretation. I, however, will not take the time to delve into such details of this caliber at present. And it is not because I am afraid; it is simply because it would be a distraction from the main points of this chapter. Though, I will admit, it takes everything in me to hold back from such a debate, as there is much I have learned on certain subjects. But maybe that is for another book, another time.

Regardless of all our differences in the Body of Christ at large, there is something to be said of the multitudes of people across the world united under His Name. Something I would say is worth a certain awe and respect. Though we have many differences in minute details of theology—such as whether the Rapture will happen or if it is even biblical (some may even be offended by me calling it a "minute" detail)—we can all, if our heart is right with God, come to agreement on the chief beliefs of Christianity. And that is a beautiful thing.

> "It is more like a hall out of which doors open into several rooms. If I can bring anyone into that hall I shall have done what I attempted. But it is in the rooms, not the hall, that there are fires and chairs and meals. The hall is a place to wait in, a place from which to try the

various doors, not a place to live in. It is true that some people may find they have to wait in the hall for a considerable time, while others feel certain almost at once which door they must knock at. I don't know why there is this difference, but I am sure that God keeps no one waiting unless He sees that it is good for him to wait. When you have reached your own room, **be kind to those who have chosen different doors and to those who are still in the hall**. If they are wrong, they need your prayers all the more; and if they are your enemies, they you are under orders to pray for them. **That is one of the rules common to the whole house.**"

-C.S. Lewis[44]

Through the Eyes of Others

It is a remarkable thing that others often have a better view of our life than we do. What I mean is this: Sometimes we are seeking answers on our own and trying to find out what we should do in certain situations, when suddenly in the midst of conversation with a friend, colleague, or mentor, it all becomes so clear. As if God were speaking directly through that person to the situation we presently face. This I believe to be partly due to the simple fact that those around us see things in our life with more clarity than we can. It seems there is a reason we can only see ourselves when looking into a mirror. This is a good thing. It calls us to be more interdependent. And God does in fact use others to speak into our lives. After all, if God can speak through the mouth of a donkey, is it really that outlandish to believe He can speak through other people? (Numbers 22:28)

There have been many occasions where I simply thought I could work out my character and decision-making processes all on my own. Just Jesus and me—that's all I thought I needed. This is an easy misconception to make. Doesn't it sound attractively pious, righteous and ultimately Christian-like? Yet, in fact, Christ said He was building His Church, His Body. This means He intends for us all to come together and support the other parts. What better way to do this than to speak to us about particular situations we face through those closest to us? Don't get me wrong; obviously we must bring everything back to the stillness before God that only comes when alone with Him. Our intimacy with Christ alone is the foundation for everything else. But this does not mean we can live a full Christian life apart from the rest of the Body.

Think about it this way: What if you cut off a piece of your own body, would it not lose its effectiveness? So it is with the Body of Christ. If we sever ourselves from the community of believers—the family we have been born into upon salvation—we will eventually lose our effectiveness in the Kingdom of God. Of course, this is also when we begin to get all kinds of strange ideas about God and theology. Allowing others into our life who will speak the truth in love to us consistently can serve as a safeguard against wrong thinking. Without this kind of protection and accountability in our lives—not to mention simple and practical insight from others—we can end up making some very ill advised decisions.

- Chapter 14 -

Pictures from Wires: Enjoy the Show

"Life is not a puzzle to be solved.

It is a mystery to be lived by faith."

-Jack Louman

- Chapter 14 -

Pictures from Wires: Enjoy the Show

We now come around full circle to where we started this journey of thought, our original analogy—one that as of yet I have not fully expounded upon: how pictures and sound ultimately come out of wires. How does TV work? How do stereos produce music for our listening pleasure? How does a cell phone or computer transmit digital information through the airwaves? Is all this even real?

I was quite curious of this question myself, as is obvious in the first chapter of this book, and so I did a little research—ironically enough, on a computer. I won't bore those of you who like me cannot handle all the details of this process. (As I was studying it, my brain began the attempt of escaping from my skull.) Those of you, who *do* have a great interest in all the details and from which your own brain will not flee, please take what I say as simply a launching point from which you can journey to more information on your own. This is of course if you do not already know all about it, in which case you may not need me to tell you again. However, I encourage you to read on all the same, as what I say after the fact may be just what you need to hear, and something you may not have thought too much about before. Let's jump right in.

Television, for instance, works by using a CRT (Cathode Ray Tube). Here is an interesting article I found about the CRT and how it works:

> In a cathode ray tube, the "cathode" is a heated filament (not unlike the filament in a normal light bulb). The heated filament is in a vacuum created inside a glass "tube." The "ray" is a stream of electrons that naturally pour off a heated cathode into the vacuum. Electrons are negative. The anode is positive, so it attracts the electrons pouring off the cathode. In a TV's cathode ray tube, the stream of electrons is focused by a focusing anode into a tight beam and then accelerated by an accelerating anode.

> This tight, high-speed beam of electrons flies through the vacuum in the tube and hits the flat screen at the other end of the tube. This screen is coated with phosphor, which glows when struck by the beam.
>
> -Marshall Brain[45]

Further information shows that the electron beam coming from the CRT must be steered by "steering coils" as when it first comes out it only hits a small area in the middle of the screen. On a black and white TV, the picture is painted on the screen line by line via this beam. On a color TV, there are actually three of these beams—red, green and blue—that move across the screen painting the picture we see. Also, a color TV differs from black and white in that instead of having only one phosphor coating, it has red, green and blue phosphor coatings in the form of lines and dots. There is also a "shadow mask" through which the beams travel before hitting the phosphor coatings.[46] But this is only regarding analog—older—televisions. These are now near obsolete as digital and HDTV's have completely taken over.

And what about stereos? How does *sound* come from wires? Basically, a speaker simply copies the electric transmission that was sent via CD, record etc. and produces physical vibrations that cause sound waves, which our eardrums then perceive as specific and detailed sounds. This all is based on the simple science of air particles pushing together, causing vibrations that eventually hit our eardrum, which then moves back and forth and interprets the vibration as sound.[47]

How, then, is digital information—especially pictures and video—appearing on our smart phones, flat screen TV's and computers possible? This is a different process entirely. All digital electronics only understand the numbers 1 and 0. Therefore, in order for digital information to travel, it is all encoded in a clever formation of these two numbers. Then, when it reaches its destination—say, from my laptop to your cell phone for instance—the recipient device would proceed to decode the cipher.[48] And this of course, all happens very quickly.

What then is the Purpose?

As I stated before, and still stand firmly upon, we do not have to understand how this phenomenon occurs in order to enjoy the results. Actually, when we know a bit more about the inner workings of technology, does it not cause even more awe? For all the elements involved in making these remarkable inventions must come from somewhere. Who invented them? Who designed them? Who gave man the intelligent ability to piece it all together into a functioning machine? Man can only take what he has been given and play around with it to invent new things. Ultimately, man creates nothing, but is simply granted by God materials with which to partake in His creative nature. It is true, however, that all we are really doing is simply putting together many things that have already been made.

To think that God is the type who would create all different kinds of elements and give us brains with which to put them together—making mind-boggling things to entertain and communicate across the globe—is a profound mystery. It is much in the same way that God created infinite space beyond earth with endless wonders simply so that we could discover amazing new things—while at the same time be kept in our place realizing we can never reach the end of it all. This is quite humbling.

When viewing all the information that I've provided on a select few forms of technology, and possibly drawing upon facts we already know about all that, an interesting question arises. Even with all that clarification—and much, much more could be made—it is still ultimately a mystery. Sure, you can explain how all the different pieces come together to make the thing work, but it doesn't do justice—that is falling short. For at the end of the day, after all the scientific studies and practical explanations, it must be admitted that no one fully understands how this occurs—or why for that matter.

If we cannot ever fully understand the basic functions of a TV screen—a piece of this physical world—how on earth could we ever fully comprehend the more supernatural elements of life, and how they work, let alone the everyday intricacies of our own lives. Truth be told, we will never be able to figure it all out. Why would we even want to? If we knew, for instance, everything that was going to happen tomorrow; if we knew all there is to know about God and all the mysteries of the universe, it wouldn't seem all that big and exciting anymore would it? Where is the sense of adventure in that? And most of all: why would we need God if we ourselves knew everything? As it is, we are not now, and never will we be, deity. We will never be omniscient and will always be dependent on God to guide us into truth. And that is a good thing.

How complex, how mysteriously wonderful are such mysteries of life—most especially the life of faith. It is important to remember that even though we cannot fully comprehend the little facets and details of how it all works, we can still enjoy the benefits produced by such processes and inner workings.

System Error

However, there is an issue we encounter with this. What if the wires (inner parts) are broken, defective even? Would it not then be necessary to find out more about the inner workings so as to fix the problem? Or further still, consult the product manual for troubleshooting, and yet further even still, if that wasn't enough, to directly contact the manufacturer for assistance—be it repairs or complete replacement with a new product.

And what if the piece of equipment—my life in this instance—I've been given did not become defective some where along the way, say, by misuse and such? What if in fact it has been defective all along? Then it may not even seem defective to me. Until the day of course when I see someone else's which is fully functional and then perceive the contrast between theirs and my own. At that time I will realize there is in fact something amiss with mine.

Or maybe it is not the seeing of someone else's life that brings me to realize my own is in disorder, but rather when I come to a place, post redemption, wherein I see the difference between my old life and new like night and day. It is much like a man who drinks cheap coffee for a long time until one day a friend gives him a taste of rich and delicious, excellently crafted coffee, thus opening his eyes to a new discovery. After tasting this decadent beverage, all the cheap coffee he used to drink no longer satisfies. He sees the contrast and realizes something is lacking, even flawed with the old stuff.

This is how it is with our analogy. We must trek far enough into understanding that we realize if something is out of place, the first step of course being salvation. But, even after one departs from the kingdom of darkness and enters the Kingdom of light, there is still much askew: a lot of habits to be broken and character to be formed over time. And though this does not mean the picture, or sound, being produced during this stage of life cannot be enjoyed, it simply means that later on that picture will be much more clear and pleasant to look at. After a good amount of time spent becoming familiar with the Manual (the Bible), and developing under the direct guidance of the Manufacturer (God), things will progressively improve in their working order. They will be aligning once again with the original purpose they were created for.

Conclusion: to be continued…

So here we are. So many facets of life, faith and philosophy have we looked upon. Yet so much is left unknown. And here begins our greatest adventure. As we choose to embark further on a journey of understanding and faith; as we encounter more obstacles; as we find more that we cannot understand; we can live what we have learned, and that which is yet unknown simply makes for more adventure.

Once we reach the end of all the discussion, analysis and exegesis we still find God. It is in fact many times at the end of such studies and endless searches for the truth that He is there, waiting. As if all the while He was saying, "If only you would have asked."

> "Call to me and I will answer you and tell you great and unsearchable things you do not know."
>
> -Jeremiah 33:3 (NIV)

Remarkably simple as it is, this is what God asks of us: childlike faith and expectancy that He will guide us in truth. What we receive in return is an endless supply of wisdom given freely. But when we ask, of course, we must not doubt. Faith does not doubt; it believes. If we think we will have a greater faith in God simply if we find out more about the world around us, and even if we study who He is in an objective manner—simply from an information-grabbing, academic standpoint—we are only fooling ourselves. As Søren Kierkegaard once said, "If I am capable of grasping God objectively, I do not believe, but precisely because I cannot do this I must believe."[49] It is in the realization that we can never "figure" God out that we realize how very real He is. And in the same stroke, we find out how real His will for our lives is.

This truth may prove quite frustrating for some, especially for those who like to have every detail of their life planned out. I'm not saying that God does not want us to make plans. I firmly believe that He does. At the same time, however, He reminds us that plans can often change. As we discussed early on in the book with the parade analogy: God can see everything all at once and thus has the ability to make the brightest judgment. We, on the other hand, often make plans that prove to be not very bright at all. But, with complete reliance on God, we have hope that even when we don't make the best plans, God will guide us to better ones.

Instead of only good ideas, they will be "God ideas", which of course are the best kinds of all.

> In his heart a man plans his course, but the LORD determines his steps
>
> -Proverbs 16:9 (NIV)

As we thoroughly discussed in earlier chapters, this does not merit inactivity on our part. We are required many times to step out in faith before we see where we are stepping, and as we step, God will reveal the way to us. He will determine our steps. Although sometimes we do see where we are stepping and we don't actually like what we see. Take for instance the story of Peter and the boat shared earlier in the book. If Peter were to focus only where he was stepping, all he would have seen were crashing waves. Not exactly the most preferable substance upon which to stand. But, at least for a moment, he kept his eyes on Christ who was summoning him onto the waves. The result: Peter walked on water. Though he didn't do it for long, the fact remains that he stepped out in an incredible leap of faith with very real results. This story proves that tangible evidence and objective truths about God aren't enough for building a solid faith. For we see later on that

Peter still denied Christ three times in a row, when in danger of a taking on a bad reputation.

Just Move

There is a phrase that I've heard preached many times that I think relates perfectly here. And though it is often frowned upon as too cliché, I think it brings some illumination. It is simply this, "God cannot steer a parked car." Not too long ago, I was having one of my more "quizzical" moments and spent a good deal of time pondering this phrase. As is necessary with many things one would like to better understand, I had to create a picture, or better yet, a scene in my mind of what this would look like. Once I'd done that I could place myself in the scene and see through the eyes of my philosophical subject. Here is the result of my thoughts.

Let's say I was sitting in my car, in a parking space at a local shopping centre. Not going anywhere, just sitting there. What happens if I start turning the steering wheel from side to side as if I were trying to get somewhere? Nothing. Sure there may be a few onlookers curious of why I am doing such a thing. Or, they may simply think it is a child waiting for their parent to return to the vehicle and pretending they're actually in a racecar—one of my favorite pastimes as a child. Other than slight vibrations the car would make with the tires vigorously shifting in place, and a few staring eyes drawn to this slight peculiarity, nothing would really happen; I wouldn't be going anywhere.

How much this is like many of us. We sit in our cars—figurative of our lives—trying desperately to imagine ourselves going somewhere. God actually wants us to move, to go places. This going requires action—faith-action. And it is in the movement, the motion, and the momentum that adventure comes into view. We cannot merely wait for the perfect circumstances. We may use excuses like, "When I have a solid career and higher income, then I can pursue God's call on my life." Or, "When I find my perfect mate, then I will step into God's plans for me." Or, "When I get out of debt…when I have less problems…when I hear an audible voice from God…then I will pursue Him and my destiny." In essence this is simply an act of frantically turning the wheels of our car (life) while sitting immobile in a parking space of sorts. We are ultimately trying to do something that only God can: "determine our steps".

We cannot figure out all the twists and turns of life. And even when—as in the actual act of driving a car—we become familiar with certain roads, we find that those roads change. There is construction, an accident, a fire or flood. We can never fully predict what we will encounter. All that we really can do is push on the gas pedal. In a way, it could be like a car that has the steering wheel on the driver's side and a gas pedal on the passenger's. God still tells us when to accelerate and when to brake, but only He can steer.

And this analogy has the same flip side to it as the other at the start of this chapter. What if there is something wrong with our vehicle? Anybody who's owned a vehicle for any length of time will be able to relate to the fact that there are endless possibilities for things going wrong (malfunctions). There are certain things that may not cause severe damage or hinder your ability to drive the vehicle—such as a scratched bumper or a small crack in your windshield. Then again there are others which, if left unchecked and unrepaired, will in fact end up causing serious damage—like a bad timing belt or a blown head gasket.

I do realize that I am sort of speaking out both sides of my mouth: saying that we should just get moving, while in the same breath, making sure that everything is in proper working order, which of course, signifies waiting, and delay. But move we must! We cannot simply sit still forever expecting God to speak with some thundering voice and until we hear such voice simply to sit on our cozy cushions of life not fulfilling His calling. But, as we move, we must have a keen ear and eye to perceive when something isn't right, and get it fixed. And believe me, if we are truly staying in constant contact with God, allowing Him to speak to us, He will let us know about the things in our lives that need repair—and even replacing.

There are no Extras

"What if God doesn't have a purpose for me?", you may ask. Possibly, you may think that others in the world were created for special purposes and you weren't. Important people of course like Pastors, Songwriters, Presidents and so on. Or maybe you do at least somewhat believe you were made for a purpose but either have no idea what that is, or simply do not have great interest in finding it out. Maybe when you think of yourself, you rather think maybe you're just a spare part in the grand scheme clockwork of the world—a piece that is only utilized when the others are all used up, when a position becomes available for you to serve and fulfill your purpose. No matter what your standpoint, and whether you agree with what I've just said or not, I leave you with a simple phrase from a film I saw recently that speaks to this perfectly. I will let this one phrase be the closing for our brief journey of thought, in hopes that it will holistically embody the message of this book: to bring encouragement and illumination…

"I'd imagine the whole world was one big machine. Machines never come with any extra parts, you know. They always come with the exact amount they need. So I figured if the entire world was one big machine, I couldn't be an extra part.

I had to be here for some reason.

And that means you have to be here for some reason too."

-Hugo Cabret, *Hugo*[50]

- Endnotes -

Preface

[1] Rottman: Carol J. Rottman, Ph.D, *Writers in the Spirit* (Grand Haven, MI: Faithwalk, 2004)

One - Childhood Ponderings

[2] Lewis: C.S. Lewis, *Mere Christianity* (New York, NY: Harper Collins, 2001), 55.

[3] Dickerson & O'Hara: Matthew T. Dickerson and David O'Hara, *From Homer to Harry Potter: A Handbook on Myth and Fantasy* (Grand Rapids, MI: Brazos, 2006), pg 80.

Two - The Unseen You

[4] Dostoyevsky: Fyodor Dostoyevsky quoted in Philip Yancey, *Rumors of Another World* (Grand Rapids, MI: Zondervan, 2003), pg 11.

[5] Myers: Allen C. Myers, *The Eerdmans Bible Dictionary* (Grand Rapids, MI: Eerdmans, 1987)

[6] Kreeft: Peter Kreeft quoted in Matthew T. Dickerson and David O'Hara, *From Homer to Harry Potter: A Handbook on Myth and Fantasy* (Grand Rapids, MI: Brazos, 2006), pg 41.

Three - Conversations with the Creator

[7] Melville: Herman Melville "Moby Dick" quoted in Joe McGinniss, *Blind Faith* (New York: Putnam, 1989).

Four - Neo-Genesis: A New Beginning

[8] Yancey: Philip Yancey, *Rumors of Another World* (Grand Rapids, MI: Zondervan, 2003), pg 100.

[9] *The Matrix* (Motion Picture). Written and directed by the Wachowski Brothers, Warner Bros. Pictures (US), 1999

[10] Yancey: Philip Yancey, *What's So Amazing About Grace* (Grand Rapids, MI: Zondervan, 1997), pg 187.

[11] Lewis: C.S. Lewis, *Mere Christianity* (New York, NY: Harper Collins, 2001)

[12] Seay & Garrett: Chris Seay and Greg Garrett, *The Gospel Reloaded* (Colorado Springs, CO: Pinon, 2003), pg 125.

Five – Through the Fog

[13] Harper: Aaron Harper, "The Fog of the Fight" viewed online at http://www.facebook.com/note.php?note_id=10150130767902224

[14] Eldredge: John Eldredge, *Wild at Heart* (Nashville, TN: Thomas Nelson, 2001)

[15] *Indiana Jones and the Last Crusade* (Motion Picture). Written by Jeffrey Boam and George Lucas, directed by Steven Spielberg, Paramount Pictures (US), 1989.

[16] Jamieson, R., Fausset, A. R., Fausset, A. R., Brown, D., & Brown, D. (1997). *A commentary, critical and explanatory, on the Old and New Testaments* (Ge 6:15). Oak Harbor, WA: Logos Research Systems, Inc.

[17] Tolkien: J.R.R. Tolkien, *The Fellowship of the Ring* (Boston: Houghton Mifflin, 1966.)

Six – The Anonymous Killer

[18] Yancey: Philip Yancey, *Rumors of Another World* (Grand Rapids, MI: Zondervan, 2003), pg 105.

[19] *Pinocchio* (Motion Picture). Written by Carlo Collodi and Tedd Sears, directed by Norman Ferguson, Walt Disney Productions (US), 1940.

[20] *The Matrix* (Motion Picture). Written and directed by the Wachowski Brothers, Warner Bros. Pictures (US), 1999.

[21] Stokes: Paul Stokes, The Telegraph, viewed online at http://www.telegraph.co.uk/news/uknews/crime/8216545/Crossb

ow-cannibal-jailed-for-wicked-and-monstrous-prostitute-murders.html

[22] London: Michael Holden London, Irish Examiner, viewed online at http://www.irishexaminer.com/sport/kfeyauauqlql/rss2/

Seven – The Anonymous Killer II: Knowing is Half the Battle

[23] "Jack the Ripper" viewed online at http://en.wikipedia.org/wiki/Jack_the_Ripper

[24] *The Last Samurai* (Motion Picture). Written by John Logan, directed by Edward Zwick, Warner Bros. Pictures (US), 2003.

Nine – The Great Beyond: The Glorious Shore

[25] "Mormons" viewed online at http://en.wikipedia.org/wiki/Mormons

[26] "Reincarnation" viewed online at

http://en.wikipedia.org/wiki/Reincarnation

[27] "Jehovah's Witnesses" viewed online at

http://en.wikipedia.org/wiki/Jehovah%27s_Witnesses

[28] Alcorn: Randy C. Alcorn, *Heaven* (Wheaton, IL: Tyndale House Publishers, Inc., 2004), pg 8.

[29] Burgess: Rt. Rev. Geo. Burgess, D. D. quoted in Rt. Rev. Samuel Fallows, D. D., *The Home Beyond: or Views of Heaven* (Detroit, MI: R.D.S. Tyler, & co., 1884), pg 404

Ten – The Great Beyond II: The Terrible Abyss

[30, 31] Bevere: John Bevere, *Driven By Eternity* (New York, NY: FaithWords, 2006)

Eleven – Head in the Clouds ~ Feet on the Ground

[32] Rabey: Steve Rabey quoted in Nancy N., "The Jesus Movement" viewed online at http://www.geftakysassembly.com/Articles/AssemblyHistory/JesusMovement.htm

[33] "talent": Thomas, R. L. (1998). *New American Standard Hebrew-Aramaic and Greek dictionaries : Updated edition*. Anaheim: Foundation Publications, Inc.

[34] Grady: J. Lee Grady, *Strange Fire in the House of God*, Charisma Magazine, viewed online at http://www.charismamag.com/index.php/fire-in-my-bones/18454-strange-fire-in-the-house-of-the-lord#comment-2049

[35] Potter: Ned Potter, "Harold Camping Predicts the End of the World, Again", ABC News, viewed online at http://abcnews.go.com/blogs/headlines/2011/10/harold-camping-predicts-end-of-the-world-again/

[36] "The Bible Guarantees It" viewed online at http://www.cbsnews.com/stories/2011/05/21/national/main20064974.shtml

Twelve – The King and His Kingdom

[37] Lewis: C.S. Lewis, *Mere Christianity* (New York, NY: Harper Collins, 2001), pg 65.

[38] McNamara: Rick McNamara, *Who Were You Expecting* viewed online at http://www.askministries.net/who-were-you-expecting/

[39] Yancey: Philip Yancey, *What's So Amazing About Grace?* (Grand Rapids, MI: Zondervan, 1997), pg 236.

Thirteen – The House

[40] "ekklēsia" 1711. Strongest NIV Exhaustive Concordance, 2nd ed. (Grand Rapids, MI: Zondervan, 1999)

[41] "oikos" 3875. Strongest NIV Exhaustive Concordance, 2nd ed. (Grand Rapids, MI: Zondervan, 1999)

[42] "oikodomeō" 3868. Strongest NIV Exhaustive Concordance, 2nd ed. (Grand Rapids, MI: Zondervan, 1999)

[43] Lewis: C.S. Lewis, *The Screwtape Letters* (New York, NY: Harper Collins, 2002), pg 129.

[44] Lewis: C.S. Lewis, *Mere Christianity* (New York, NY: Harper Collins, 2001), Preface.

Fourteen – Pictures from Wires: Enjoy the Show

[45] Brain: Marshall Brain, "How Television Works" viewed online at http://electronics.howstuffworks.com/tv3.htm

[46] Brain: Marshall Brain, "How Television Works" viewed online at http://electronics.howstuffworks.com/tv10.htm

[47] Harris: Tom Harris, "How Speakers Work" viewed online at http://electronics.howstuffworks.com/speaker1.htm

[48] Brain: Marshall Brain, "How Bits and Bytes Work" viewed online at http://computer.howstuffworks.com/bytes1.htm

[49] Soren Kierkegaard. (n.d.). BrainyQuote.com. Retrieved February 18, 2012, from BrainyQuote.com Web site: http://www.brainyquote.com/quotes/quotes/s/sorenkierk388886.html

[50] *Hugo* (Motion Picture). Written by John Logan and Brian Selznick, directed by Martin Scorsese, Paramount Pictures (US), 2011.

ABOUT THE AUTHOR

P.M. Stuebe received his Associate of Theology degree [Summa Cum Laude] from Portland Bible College in Spring of 2011. He served as a leader at True Life Fellowship and City Bible Church for several years, mainly working with youth and young adults: leading small groups; preaching and teaching. He has authored a non-fiction *Into the Unknown* and is currently writing a fantasy series entitled *Epoch*. He anticipates finishing the first book in the series by early 2014. Aside from authoring full-length books, he also spends time in poetry and songwriting. Originally from the Greater Portland Area, Stuebe relocated to Canada in 2013. He and his wife Megan live in southwestern British Columbia.

Made in the USA
Charleston, SC
13 April 2013